www.ingramcontent.com/pod-product-compliance
Lightning Source LLC
Chambersburg PA
CBHW081515040426
42447CB00013B/3234

بیایید کلمه های فارسی بیاموزیم

(تمرین های کمک درسی)

کتاب اوّل

Let's Learn Persian Words

A Farsi Activity Book

Book One

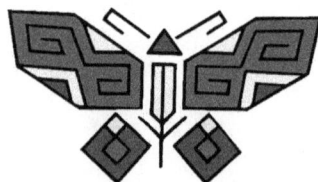

Bahar Books

www.baharbooks.com

Mirsadeghi, Nazanin
    Let's Learn Persian Words: A Farsi Activity Book - Book One / Nazanin Mirsadeghi

ISBN-10: 1939099005
ISBN-13: 978-1-939099006

Published by Bahar Books, White Plains, New York

بیایید کلمه های فارسی بیاموزیم

Let's Learn Persian Words

سخنی با خوانندگان فارسی زبان ،

یکی از مشکلات آموزش زبان فارسی به کودکانی که فارسی را به عنوان زبان دوّم می آموزند ، دسترسی نداشتن به کتاب های کمک درسی ای ست که برای این دسته از دانش آموزان طرح– ریزی شده باشند.

هدف اصلی این مجموعه (کتاب اوّل و کتاب دوّم) ، فراهم آوردن تمرین هایی ست که با روش تدریس کتاب ''آموزش زبان فارسی اوّل دبستان'' – که منبع اصلی تدریس در اکثر مدرسه های فارسی در خارج از کشورست – هماهنگی داشته و در ضمن با کمک گیری از بازی ها و جدول ها، یادگیری خواندن و نوشتن کلمات تازه را برای دانش آموزان ساده تر کنند.

ترتیب حروف استفاده شده در این کتاب ها هماهنگ با ترتیب تدریس این حروف در کتاب ''آموزش زبان فارسی اوّل دبستان'' است. به همین دلیل، این کتاب و سایر کتاب های این مجموعه می توانند به عنوان تمرینات اضافه در کنار کتاب اصلی آموزش زبان فارسی توسط آموزگاران و پدران و مادران دانش آموزان مورد استفاده قرار گیرند.

در اینجا لازم می دانم از خانم لادن مشتاقی که با نظرات و پیشنهادات شان من را در کار تنظیم این کتاب یاری دادند صمیمانه سپاسگزاری کنم.

نازنین میرصادقی

To English-speaking readers ...

The activity books in this series (Book One & Book Two) have been designed for students of Iranian Heritage who are learning Persian as a second language in a classroom. These activity books could be used as a supplement to the *Elementary Persian Language* textbook which is the main resource used in most Persian schools outside Iran. The letters used in each activity in this series are sequenced in the same order as the letters taught in the *Elementary Persian Language* textbook.

If you are learning Persian on your own, you should be familiar with the Persian alphabet and be able to read the Persian script prior to using these workbooks. These practical activity books could provide you with fun and effective ways to expand your reading and writing vocabulary through a variety of activities such as puzzles, word searches and matching exercises.

Many Thanks are due to Mrs. Ladan Moshtaghi for her help and support in preparing these books.

Nazanin Mirsadeghi

Pronunciation Guide for the Persian Letters

aa like the "a" in arm	* آ – ا
b like the "b" in boy	ب – بـ
p like the "p" in play	پ – پـ
t like the "t" in tree	ت – تـ
s like the "s" in sun	ث – ثـ
j like the "j" in jam	ج – جـ
ch like the "ch" in child	چ – چـ
h like the "h" in hotel	ح – حـ
ǩ like "ch" in the German word *bach*, or Hebrew word *smach*.	خ – خـ
d like the "d" in door	د
z like the "z" in zebra	ذ
r like the "r" in rabbit	ر
z like the "z" in zebra	ز
ž like the "z" in zwago	ژ
s like the "s" in sun	س – سـ
sh like the "sh" in shell	ش – شـ
s like the "s" in sun	ص – صـ
z like the "z" in zebra	ض – ضـ
t like the "t" in tree	ط
z like the "z" in zebra	ظ

' is a glottal stop, like between the syllables of "uh-oh"	ع – � – ﻉ
ğ like the "r " in French word *merci*	غ – ﻐ – ﻎ
f like the "f " in fall	ﻓ – ف
ğ like the "r" in French word *merci*	ﻗ – ق
k like the "k" in kite	ﻛ – ک
g like the "g" in game	ﮔ – گ
l like the "l" in lost	ﻟ – ل
m like the "m" in master	ﻣ – م
n like the "n" in night	ﻧ – ن
v like the "v" in van	و
o like the "o" in ocean	و
On some occasions, it has no sound and becomes silent.	و
oo like the "oo" in good	* او – و
h like the "h" in hotel	ه – ﺤ – ﻬ – ﮬ
e like the "e" in element	ه – ﻪ
y like the "y" in yellow	ﻳ – ی
ee like the "ee" in need	* ايـ – يـ – ی – ای

* long vowels

It represents doubled consonants.	ـّ
a like the "a" in animal	ـَ – اَ **
o like the "o" in ocean	ـُ – اُ **
e like the "e" in element	ـِ – اِ **

** short vowels

Persian Letters with the Same Pronunciation

t like the "t" in tree	ﺕ – ﻁ
	ﻁ
ğ like the "r" in French word *merci*	ﻕ – ﻕ
	ﻍ – ﻎ – ﻍ
h like the "h" in hotel	ﺡ – ﺡ
	ﻩ – ﻪ – ﻬ – ﻩ
s like the "s" in sun	ﺙ – ﺙ
	ﺱ – ﺱ
	ﺹ – ﺹ
z like the "z" in zebra	ﺫ
	ﺯ
	ﺽ
	ﻅ

Names Given to the Persian Letters

alef	آ – ا
be	بـ – ب
pe	پـ – پ
te	تـ – ت
se	ثـ – ث
jeem	جـ – ج
che	چـ – چ
he	حـ – ح
ǩe	خـ – خ
daal	د
zaal	ذ
re	ر
ze	ز
že	ژ
seen	سـ – س
sheen	شـ – ش
saad	صـ – ص
zaad	ضـ – ض
taa	ط
zaa	ظ

eyn	ع - ع - ء
ğeyn	غ - غ - غ
fe	ف - ف
ğaaf	ق - ق
kaaf	ک - ک
gaaf	گ - گ
laam	ل - ا
meem	م - م
noon	ن - ن
vaav	و
he	ه - ه - ه - ه
ye	ی - ی

حروف به کار گرفته شده در تمرین های این کتاب

Letters Used in This Book's Activities

** اِ - اـ	* آ - ا - ا
ش - شـ	ب - بـ
ی - یـ y like the "y" in yellow	** اَ - اـ َ
** اُ - اـ ُ	د
ک - کـ	م - مـ
و v like the "v" in van	س - سـ
پ - پـ	* او - و oo like the "oo" in good
گ - گـ	ت - تـ
ف - فـ	ر
خ - خـ	ن - نـ
	* ای - یـ - ی - ای ee like the "ee" in need
	ز
	ه - هـ e like the "e" in element

*   long vowels

** short vowels

Exercise 1

تمرین ۱

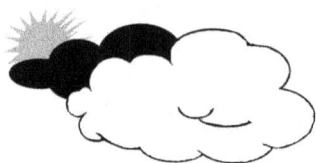

Clouds

آبر

(abr)

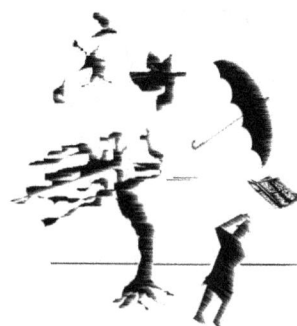

Wind

باد

(baad)

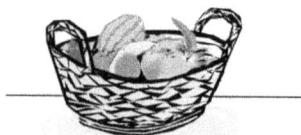

Basket

سَبَد

(sa. bad)

Read the word for each picture and
write the letters in their places.

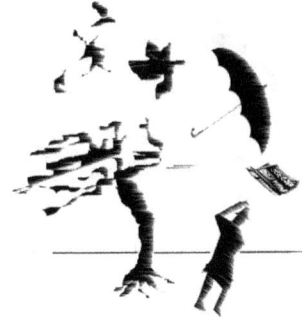

Wind

باد

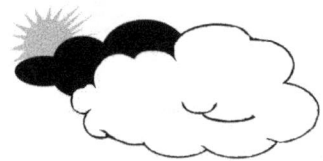

Clouds

آبر

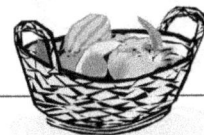

Basket

سَبَد

۱۴

Connect each word to its picture.

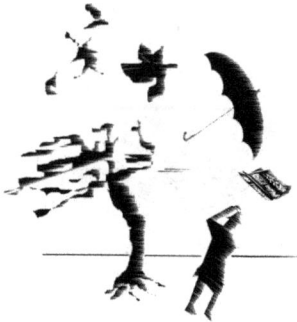

Wind

سَبَد

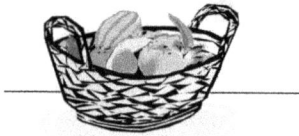

Basket

آبر

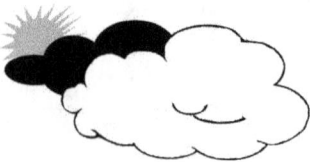

Clouds

باد

Read the word for each picture and
write the letters in the puzzle.

با کمکِ شکل ها، هر کلمه را بخوان و
جایش را در جدول پیدا کن.

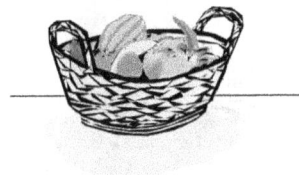

Basket

سَبَد

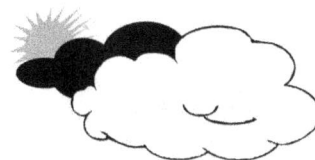

Clouds

آبر

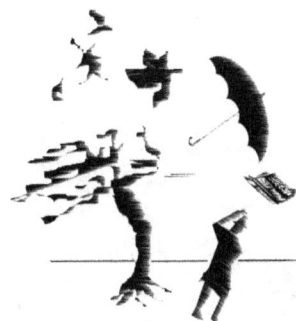

Wind

باد

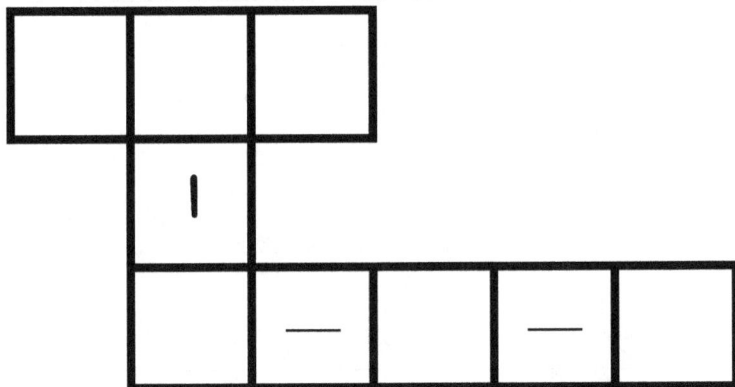

Find the word below in the puzzle.

کلمه زیر را در جدول پیدا کن.

سَبَد

م	ا	ل	سَ	پ	ص	ن
چ	د	ا	بَ	ا	ب	ج
ا	بُ	ث	د	ت	ى	ا
ن	ا	شَ	ط	بَ	ه	ل
ص	ف	ا	ع	ن	و	ا

Look at this picture and write its name under it. به این شکل نگاه کن و اسمش را زیر آن بنویس.

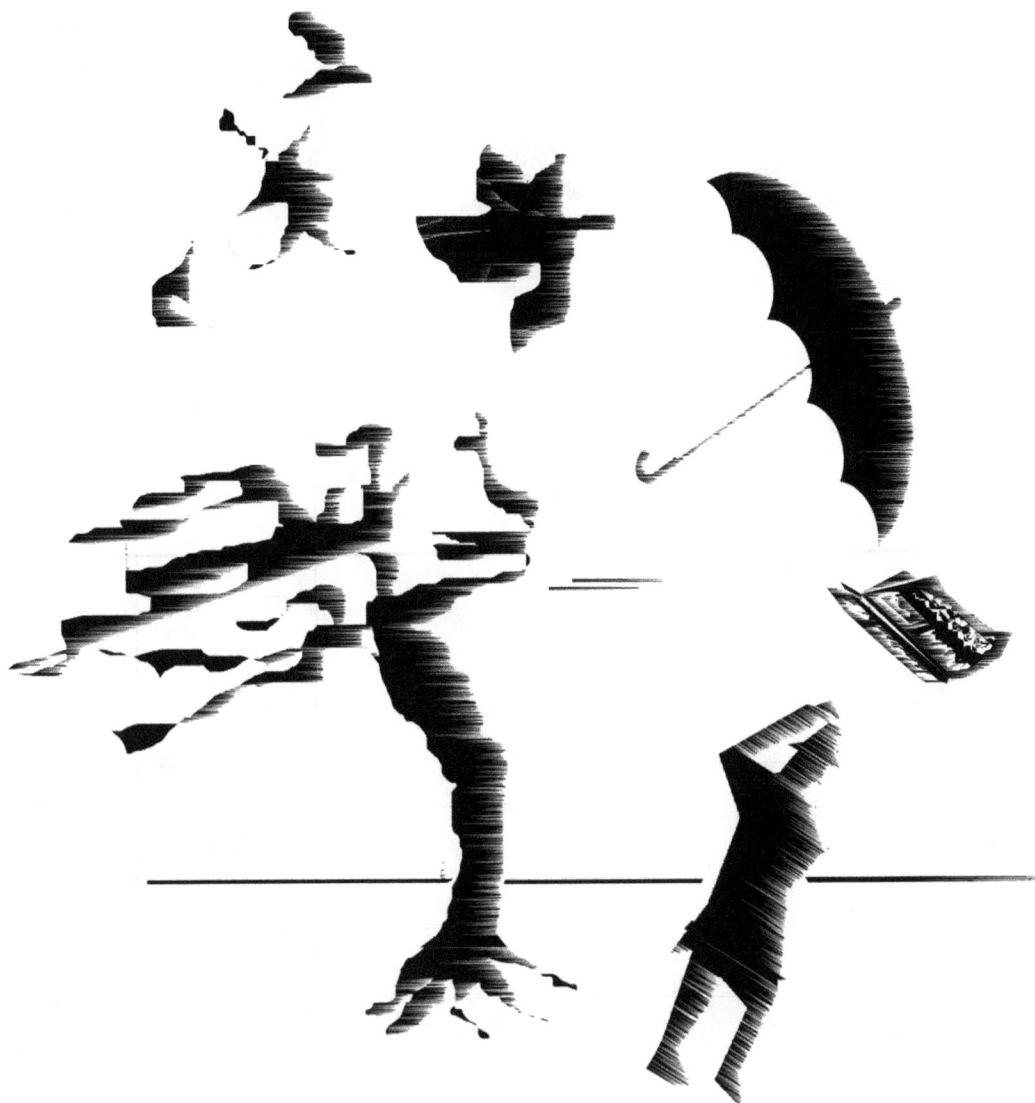

Wind

_____

Write the letters for each word.

صداهای هر کلمه را بنویس.

آبَر = __ + __ + __

باد = __ + __ + __

سَبَد = __ + __ + __ + __ + __

آبر

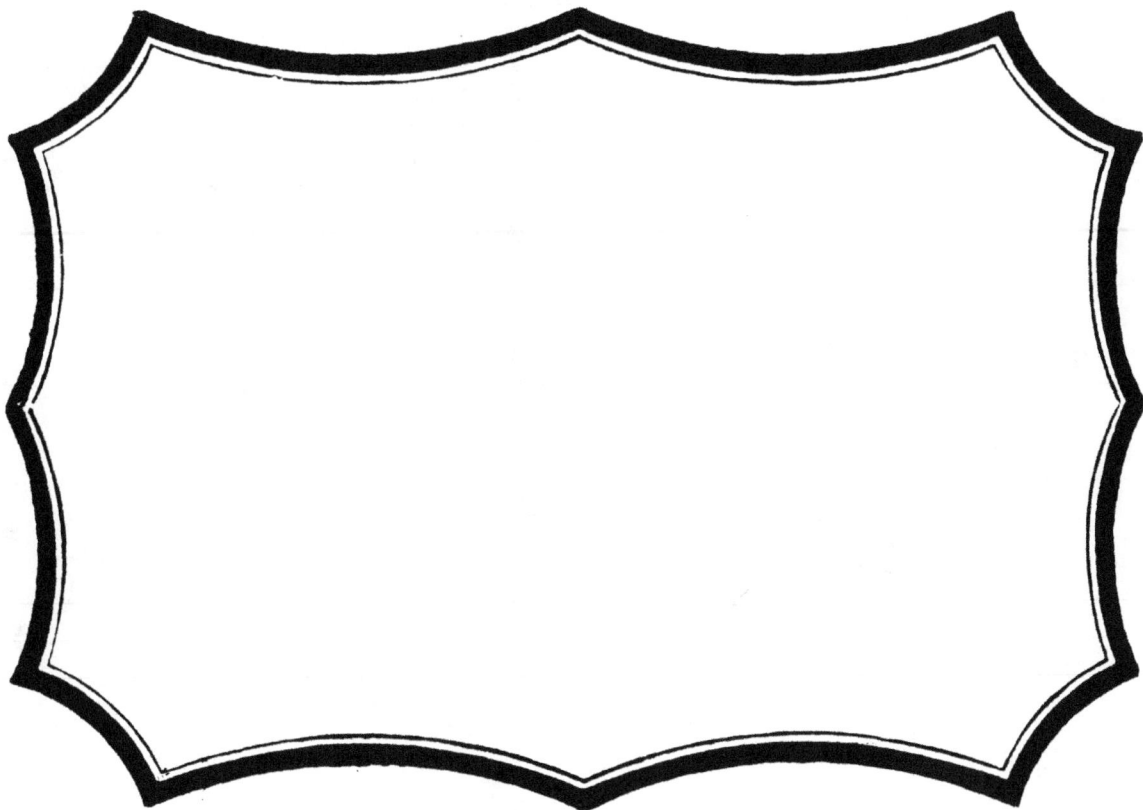

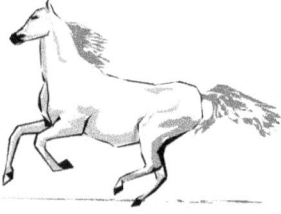

Horse

آسب

(asb)

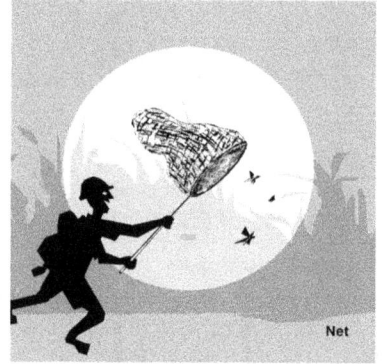

Net

تور

(toor)

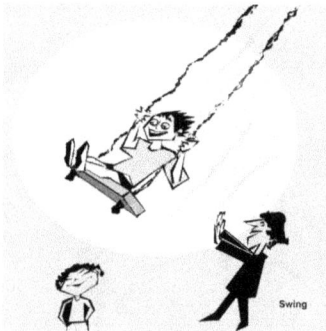

Swing

تاب

(taab)

Read the word for each picture and write the letters in their places.

با کمک شکل ها، هر کلمه را بخوان و صداهایش را در جدولِ روبرویش بنویس.

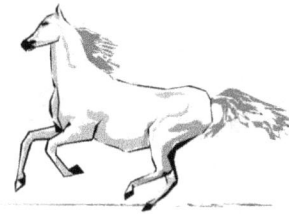

Horse

آسب

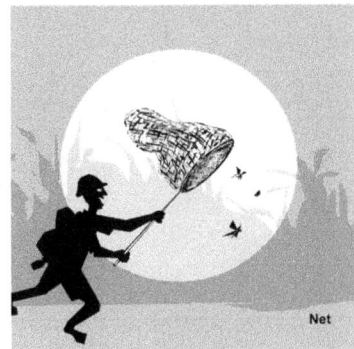

Net

تور

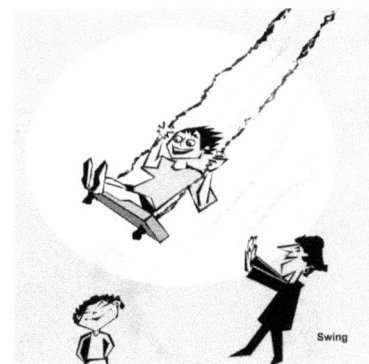

Swing

تاب

۲۲

Connect each word to its picture.

هر کلمه را به شکلش وصل کن.

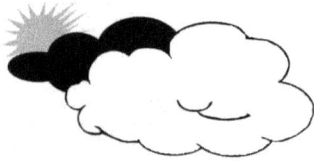
Clouds

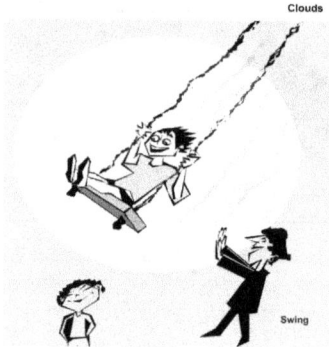
Swing

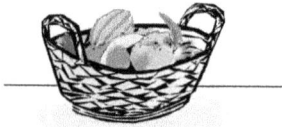
Basket

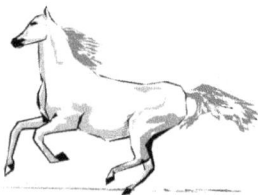
Horse

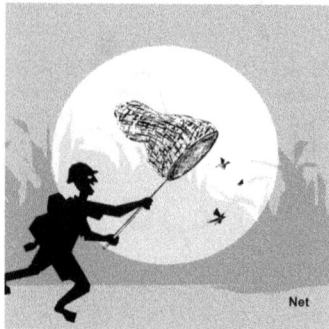
Net

تور

آسب

تاب

آبر

سَبَد

Read the word for each picture and
write the letters in the puzzle.

با کمکِ شکل ها، هر کلمه را بخوان و
جایش را در جدول پیدا کن.

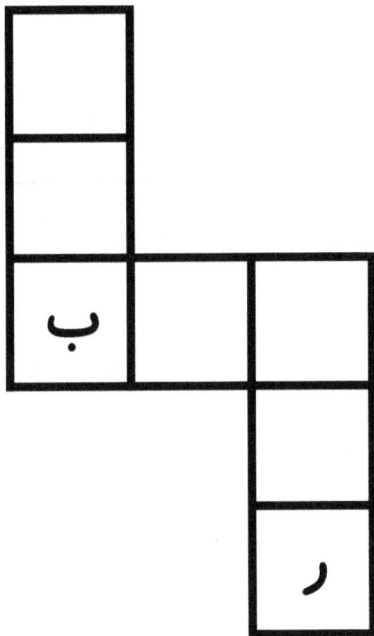

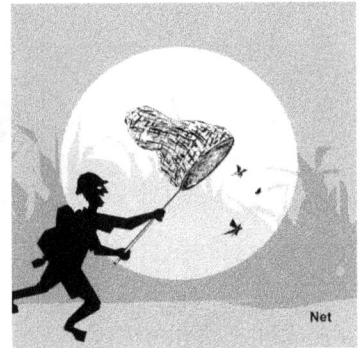

تور

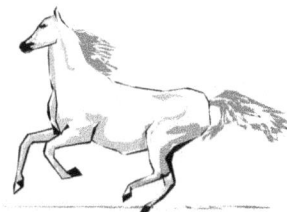

آسب

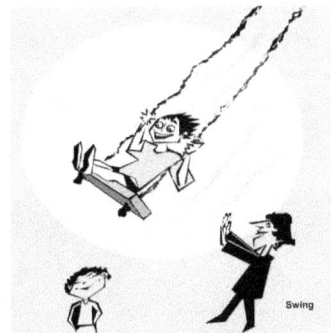

تاب

Find the word below in the puzzle.

کلمه زیر را در جدول پیدا کن.

آسب

ه	ض	ت	ر	ی	سَ
و	ط	اَ	س	ب	ا
سُ	د	ی	اِ	ل	وَ
و	چ	ف	ش	ا	ک

Look at this picture and write its name under it.   به این شکل نگاه کن و اسمش را زیر آن بنویس.

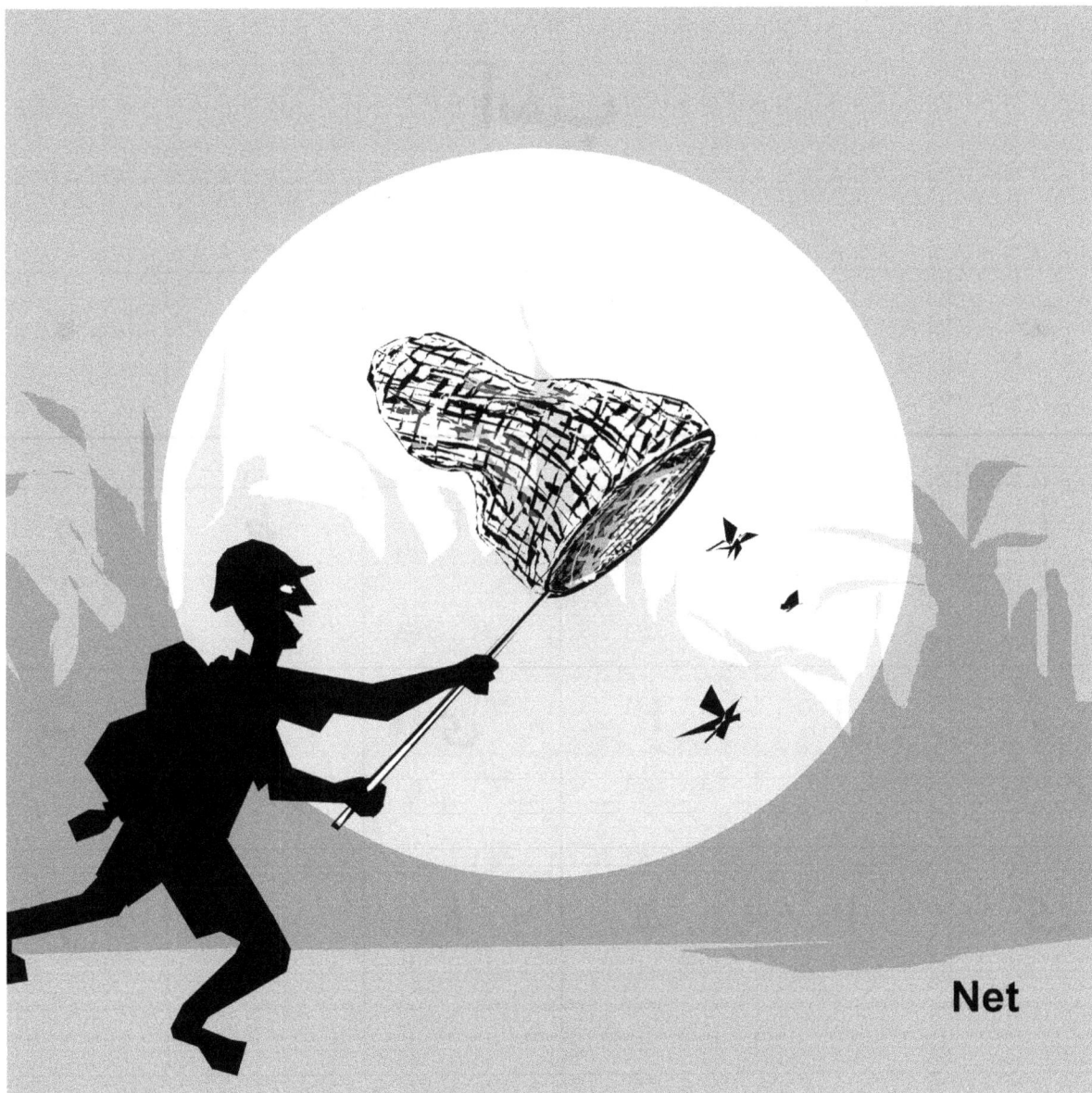

Net

_____

Write the letters for each word.   صداهای هر کلمه را بنویس.

آسب = ___ + ___ + ___

تور = ___ + ___ + ___

تاب = ___ + ___ + ___

Read the word below and draw a picture of it.	کلمه زیر را بخوان و شکلش را بکش.

تاب

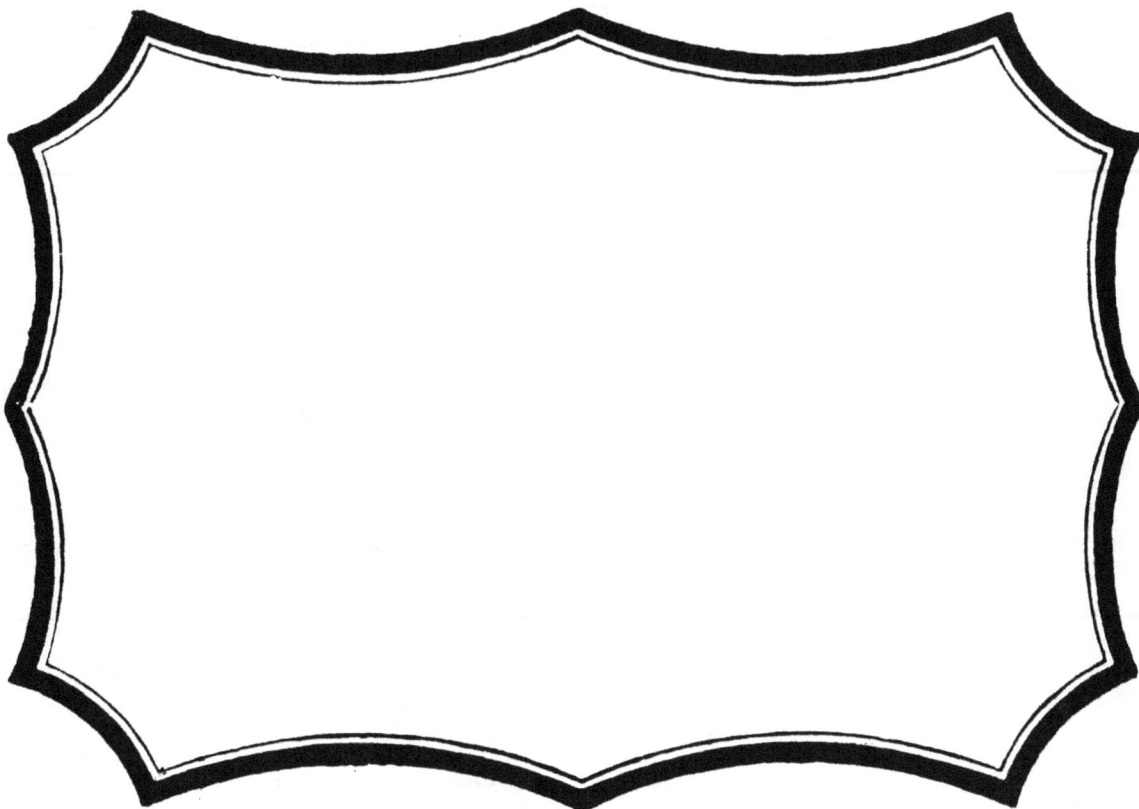

Exercise 3

تمرین ۳

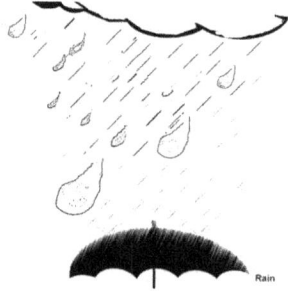

Rain

باران

(baa. raan)

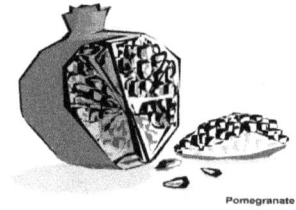

Pomegranate

آنار

(a. naar)

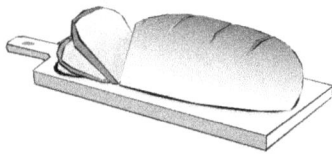

Bread

نان

(naan)

Read the word for each picture and
write the letters in their places.

با کمک شکل ها، هر کلمه را بخوان و
صداهایش را در جدولِ روبرویش بنویس.

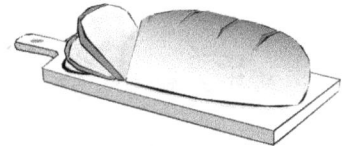

Bread

نان

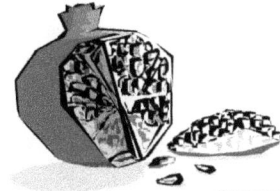

Pomegranate

آنار

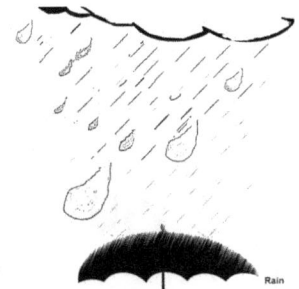

Rain

باران

Connect each word to its picture.

هر کلمه را به شکلش وصل کن.

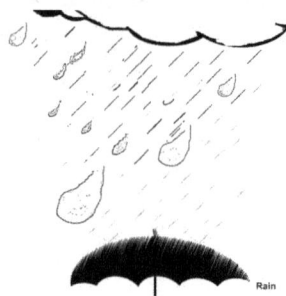
Rain

آنار

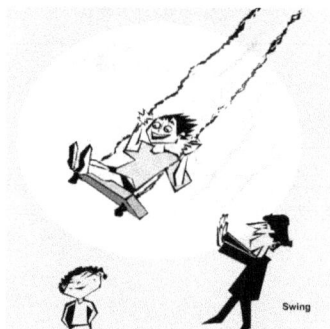
Swing

نان

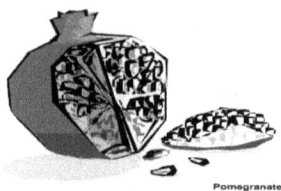
Pomegranate

تاب

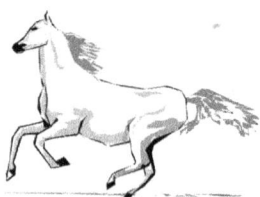
Horse

باران

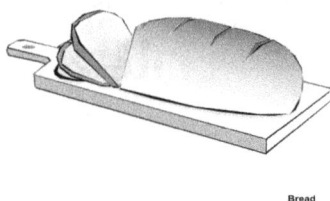
Bread

اَسب

Read the word for each picture and
write the letters in the puzzle.

با کمکِ شکل ها، هر کلمه را بخوان و
جایش را در جدول پیدا کن.

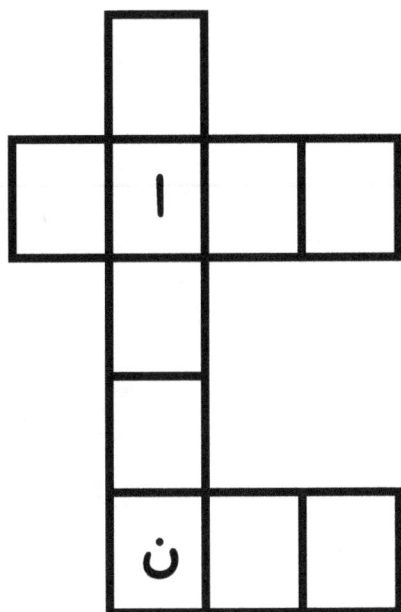

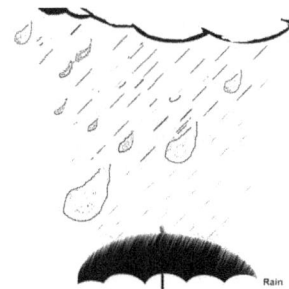

باران

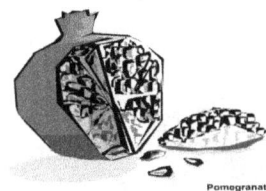

آنار

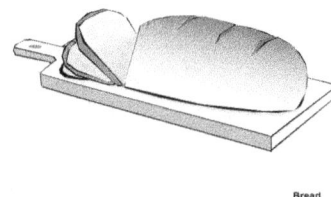

نان

Find the word below in the puzzle.

کلمه زیر را در جدول پیدا کن.

نان

ت	و	ف	ن	ا	ت
ا	ش	ذ	ر	ی	ق
ز	گ	ا	ی	ن	ک
ب	و	ن	ه	خ	ل

Look at this picture and write its name under it.   به این شکل نگاه کن و اسمش را زیر آن بنویس.

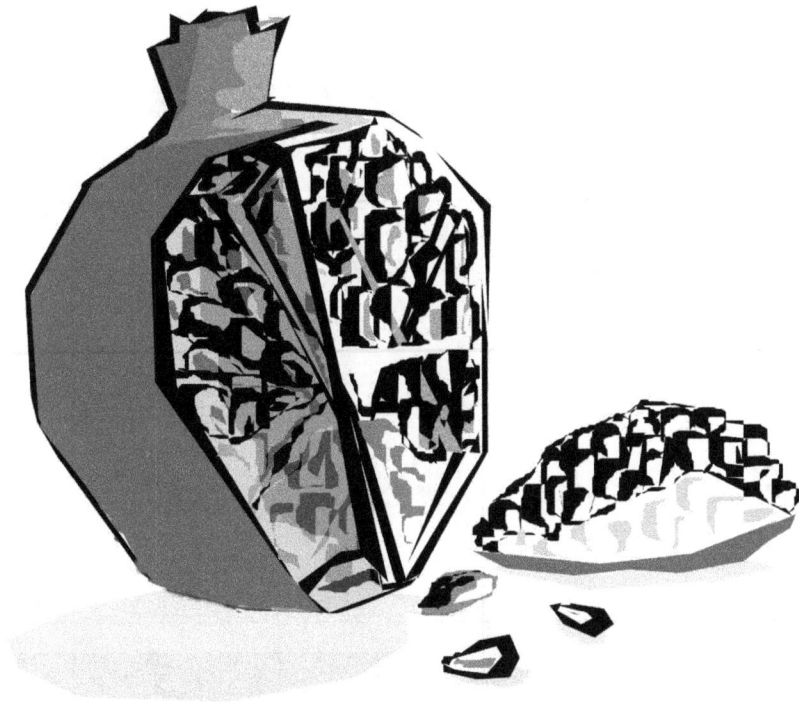

Pomegranate

——————————————

Write the letters for each word.

صداهای هر کلمه را بنویس.

نان= __ + __ + __

آنار= __ + __ + __ + __

باران= __ + __ + __ + __ + __

Read the word below and draw a picture of it. کلمه زیر را بخوان و شکلش را بکش.

باران

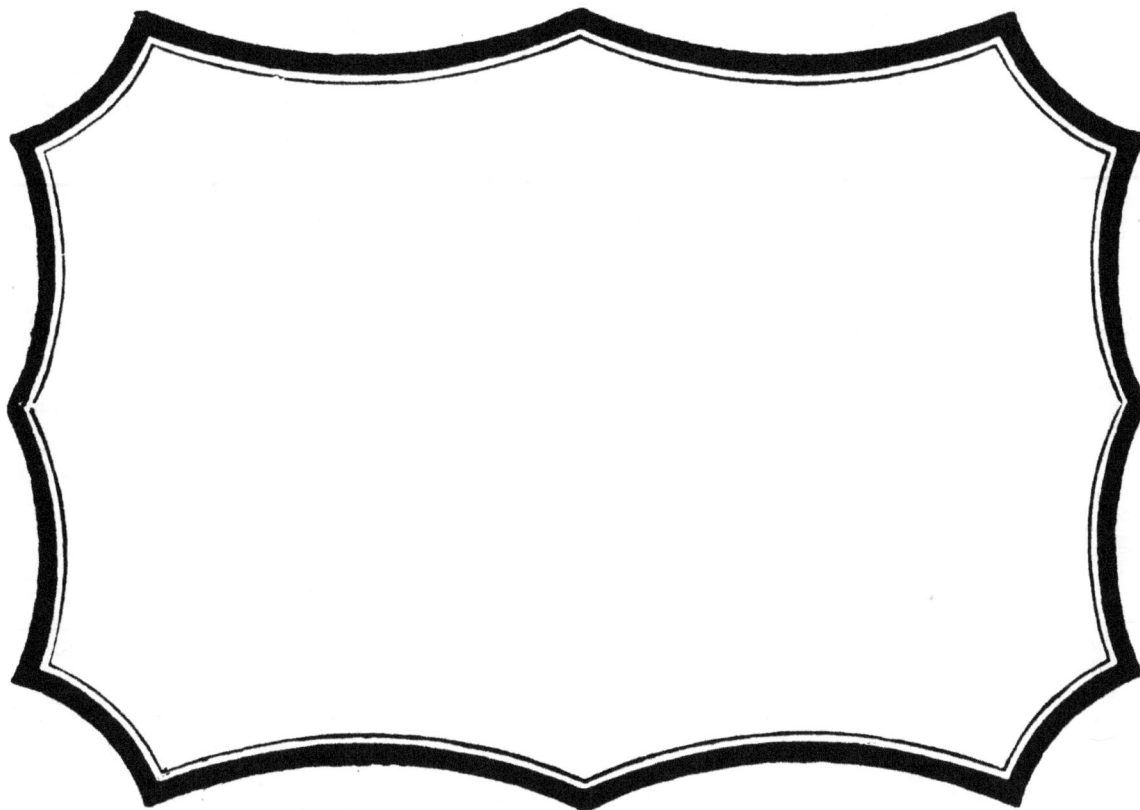

Exercise 4

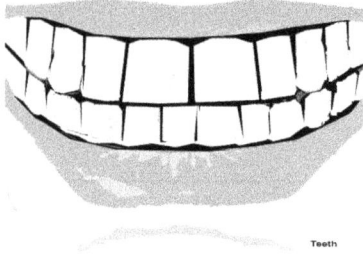

دَندان

(dan. daan)

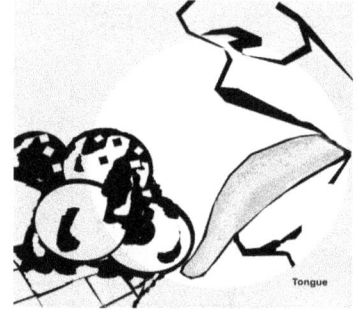

زَبان

(za. baan)

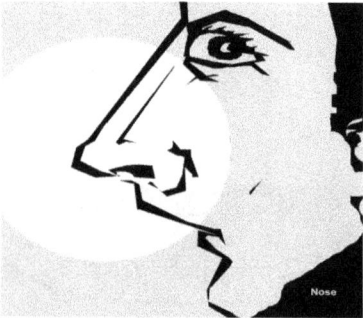

بینی

(bee. nee)

Read the word for each picture and
write the letters in their places.

با کمک شکل ها، هر کلمه را بخوان و
صداهایش را در جدولِ روبرویش بنویس.

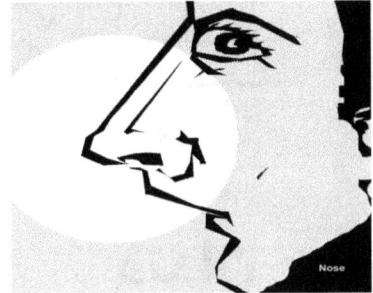

بینی

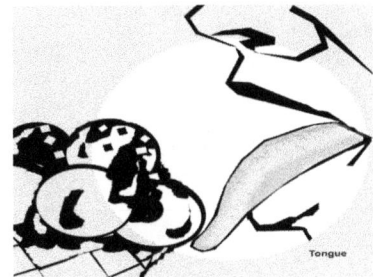

زَبان

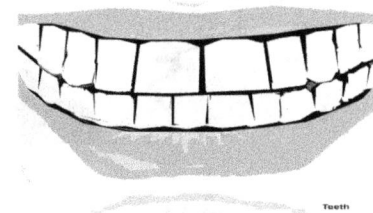

دَندان

Connect each word to its picture.   هر کلمه را به شکلش وصل کن.

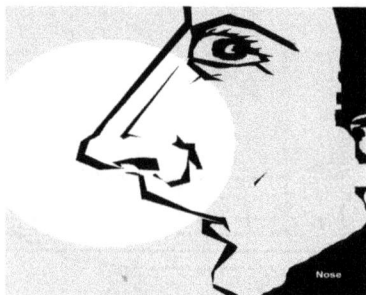

زَبان

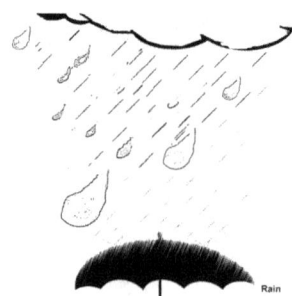

نان

دَندان

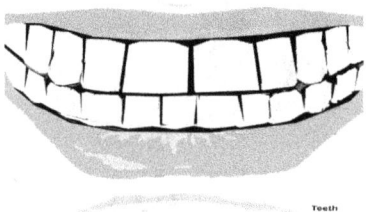

باران

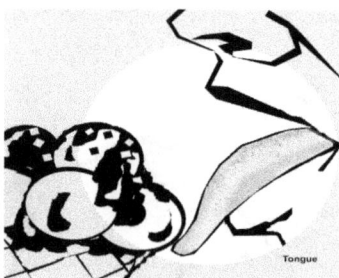

بینی

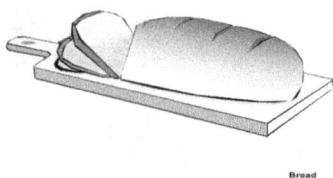

Read the word for each picture and
write the letters in the puzzle.

با کمک شکل ها، هر کلمه را بخوان و
جایش را در جدول پیدا کن.

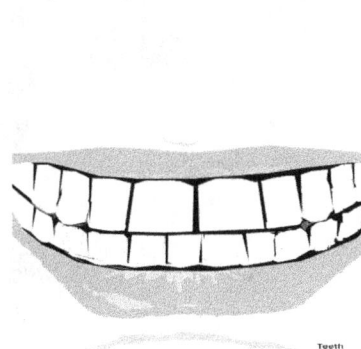

دَندان

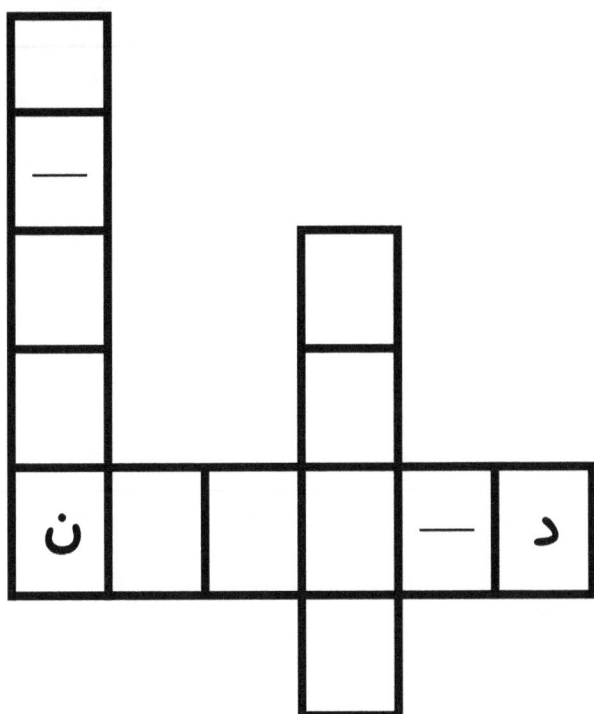

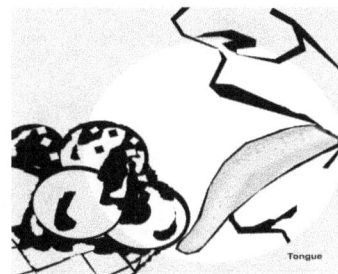

زَبان

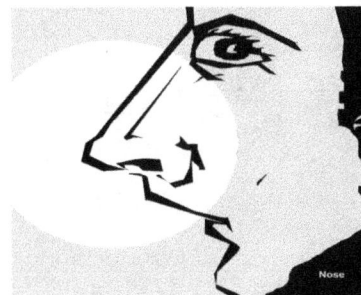

بینی

Find the word below in the puzzle.   کلمه زیر را در جدول پیدا کن.

بینی

ذ	پ	ف	ن	ز	س
ا	بِ	یِ	ذِ	ی	ب
م	ذِ	ا	و	دَ	ش
ا	خ	ل	دَ	ذِ	ز

۴۱

به این شکل نگاه کن و اسمش را زیر شکل بنویس. Look at this picture and write its name under it.

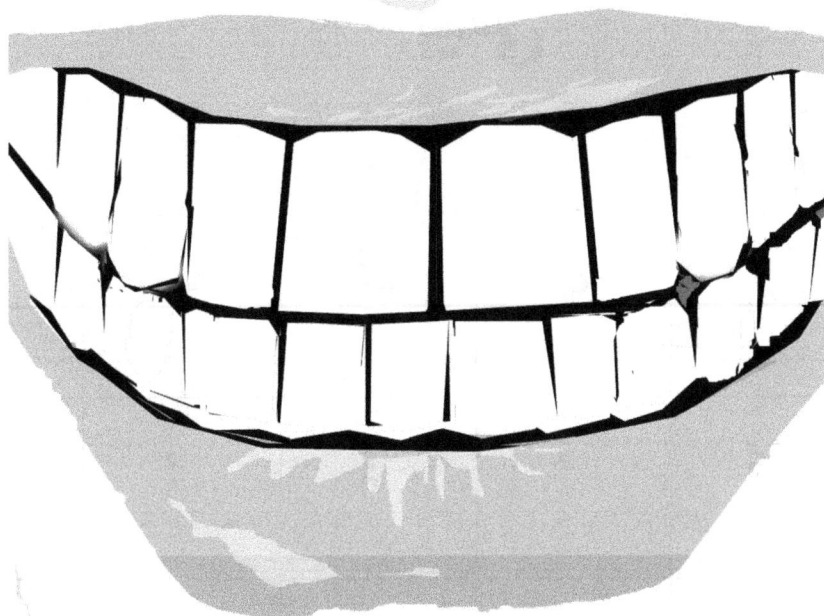

Teeth

_____

Write the letters for each word.

صداهای هر کلمه را بنویس.

بینی = __ + __ + __ + __

زَبان= __ + __ + __ + __ + __

دَندان= __ + __ + __ + __ + __ + __ + __

Read the word below and draw a picture of it.   کلمه زیر را بخوان و شکلش را بکش.

زَبان

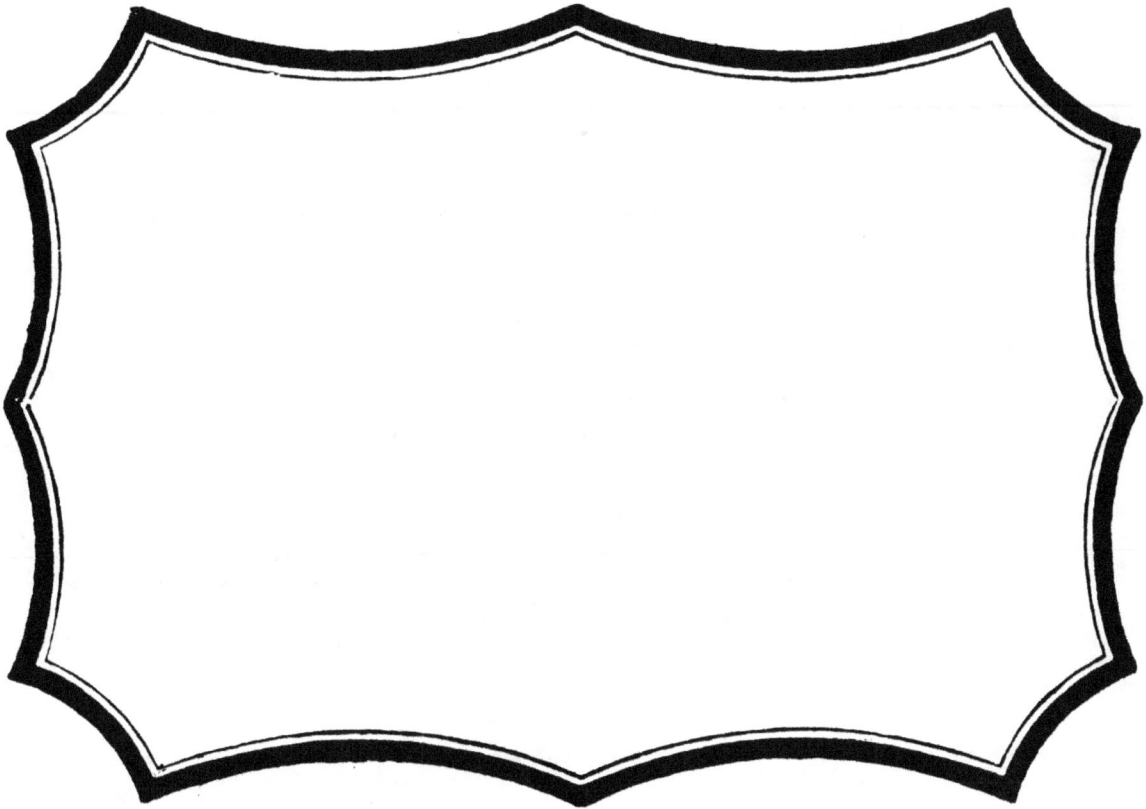

Exercise 5

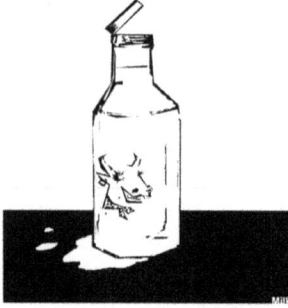

شیر

(sheer)

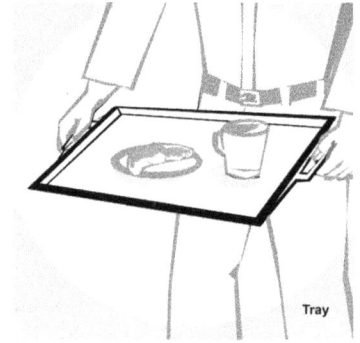

سینی

(see. nee)

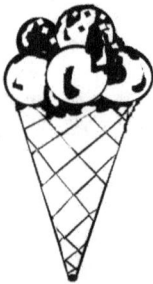

بَستَنی

(bas. ta. nee)

Read the word for each picture and
write the letters in their places.

با کمک شکل ها، هر کلمه را بخوان و
صداهایش را در جدولِ روبرویش بنویس.

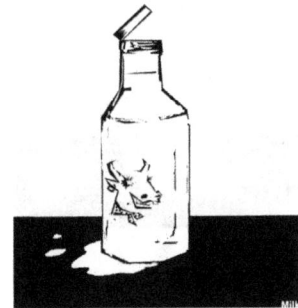

شیر

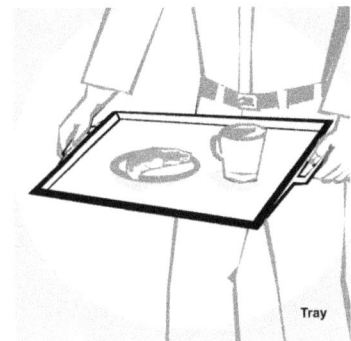

Tray

سینی

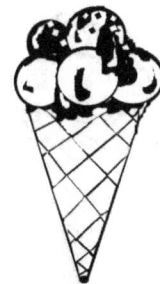

Ice Cream

بَستَنی

Connect each word to its picture.

هر کلمه را به شکلش وصل کن.

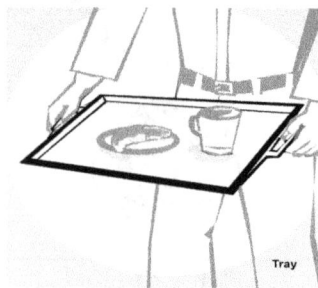
Tray

زَبان

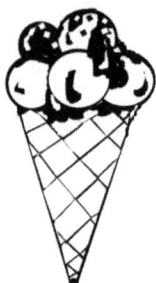
Ice Cream

شیر

دَندان

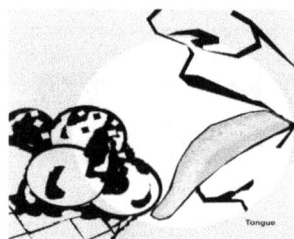
Tongue

بَستَنی

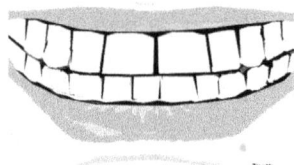
Teeth

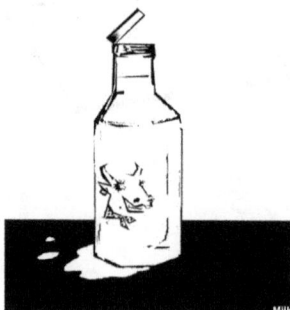
Milk

سینی

Read the word for each picture and write the letters in the puzzle.

با کمک شکل ها، هر کلمه را بخوان و جایش را در جدول پیدا کن.

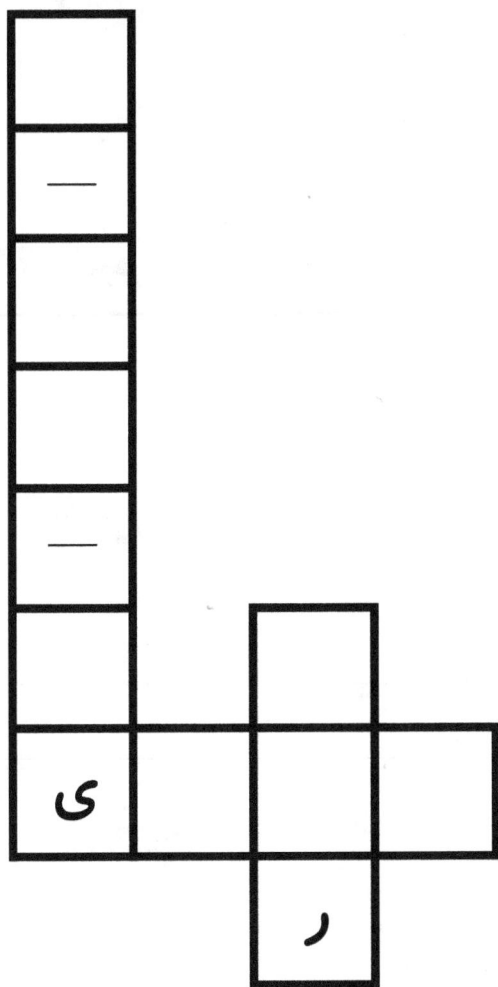

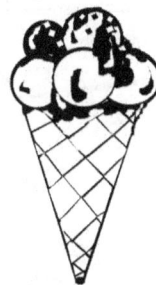

Ice Cream

بَستَنی

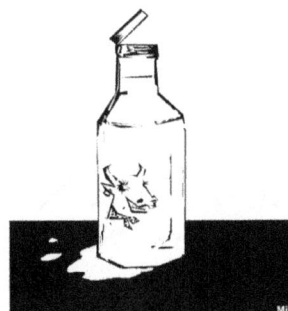

Milk

شیر

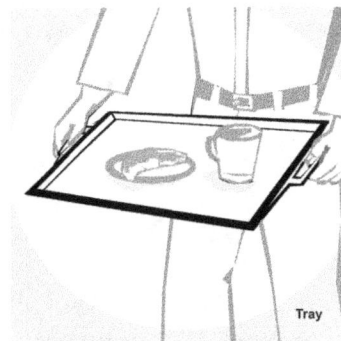

Tray

سینی

سینی

ط	ی	غ	ه	ا	ش	ت
ذ	س	اُ	دَ	ز	و	ا
ف	یـ	و	ب	ا	ل	ش
پِ	ن	ی	ذ	یـ	سـ	و
گ	ســ	و	ا	ل	م	ا

Look at this picture and write its name under it. به این شکل نگاه کن و اسمش را زیر شکل بنویس.

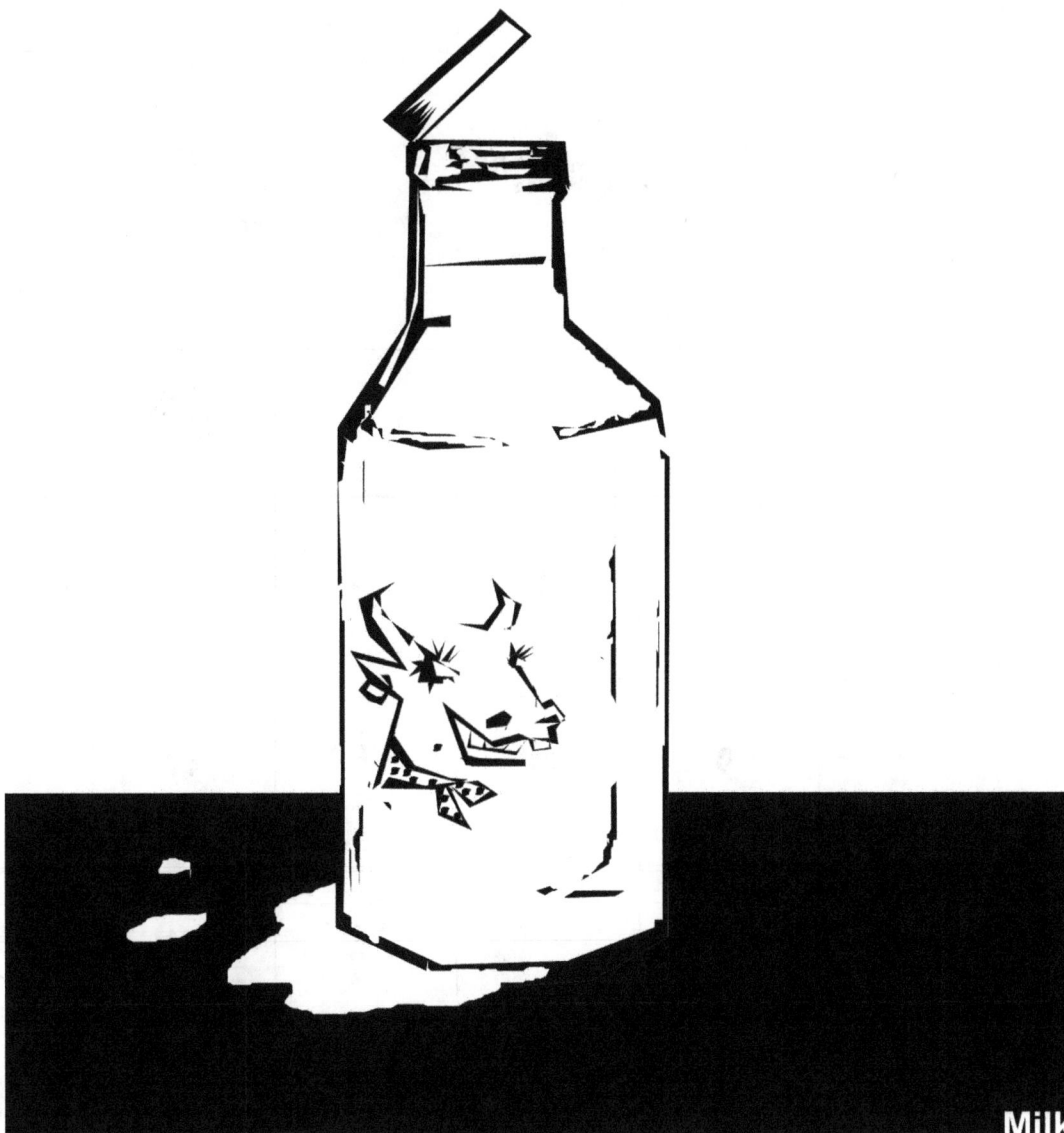

Milk

_____

Write the letters for each word.

صداهای هر کلمه را بنویس.

شیر = __ + __ + __

سینی = __ + __ + __ + __

بَستَنی = __ + __ + __ + __ + __ + __ + __

Read the word below and draw a picture of it. کلمه زیر را بخوان و شکلش را بکش.

بَستَنی

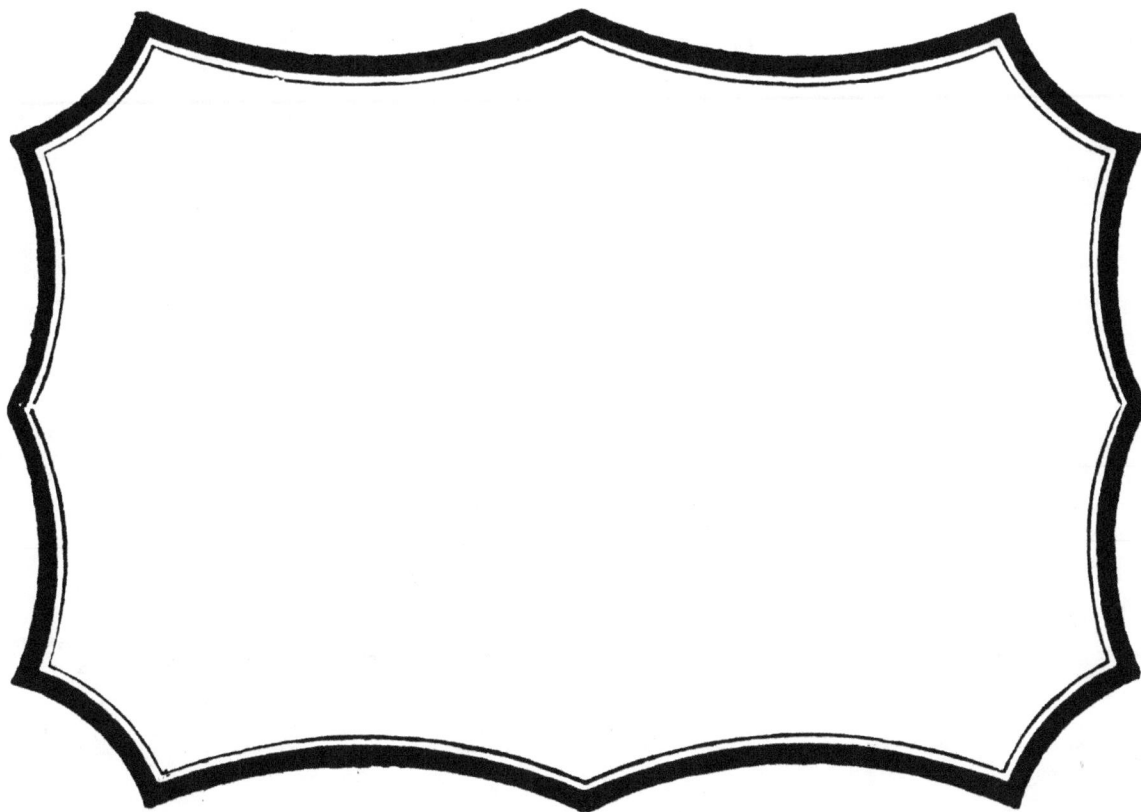

Exercise 6

تمرین ۶

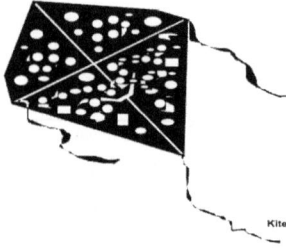

بادبادَک

(baad. baa. dak)

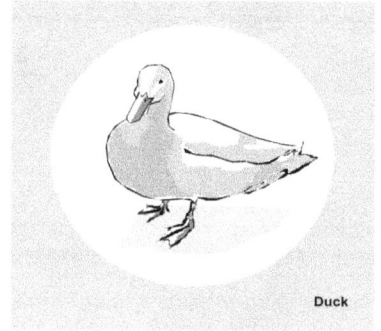

Duck

اُردَک

(or. dak)

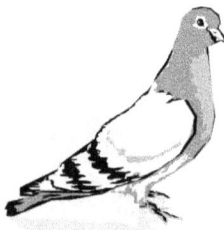

Pigeon

کَبوتَر

(ka. boo. tar)

Read the word for each picture and
write the letters in their places.

با کمک شکل ها، هر کلمه را بخوان و
صداهایش را در جدولِ روبرویش بنویس.

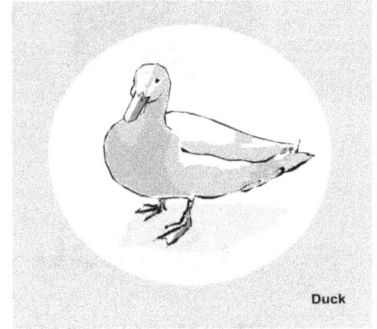

Duck

اُردَک

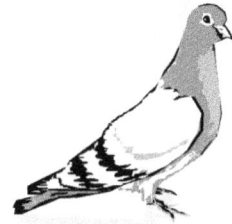

Pigeon

کَبوتَر

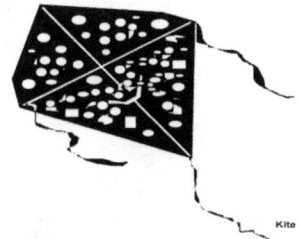

Kite

بادبادَک

Connect each word to its picture.

هر کلمه را به شکلش وصل کن.

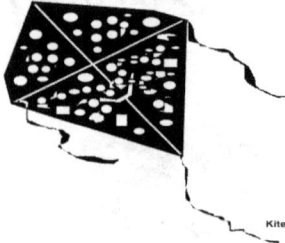

Kite

کَبوتَر

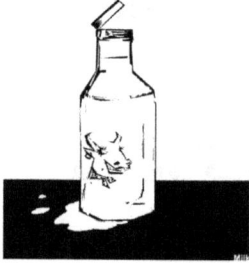

Milk

بَستَنی

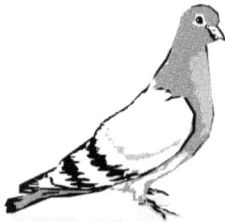

Pigeon

بادبادَک

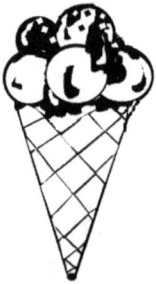

Ice Cream

شیر

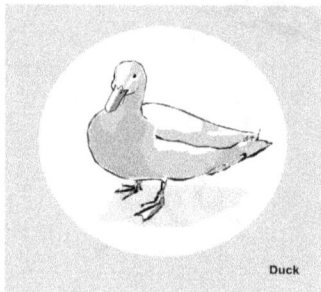

Duck

اُردَک

Read the word for each picture and
write the letters in the puzzle.

با کمک شکل ها، هر کلمه را بخوان و جایش را در جدول پیدا کن.

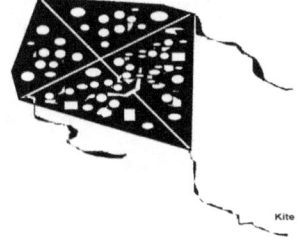

بادبادَک

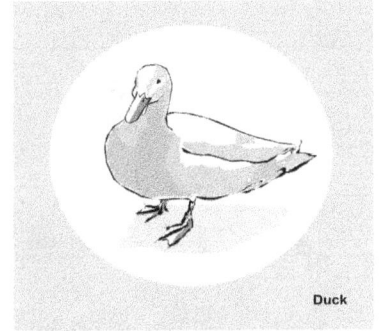

اُردَک

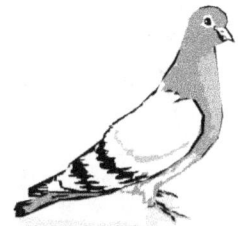

گَبوتَر

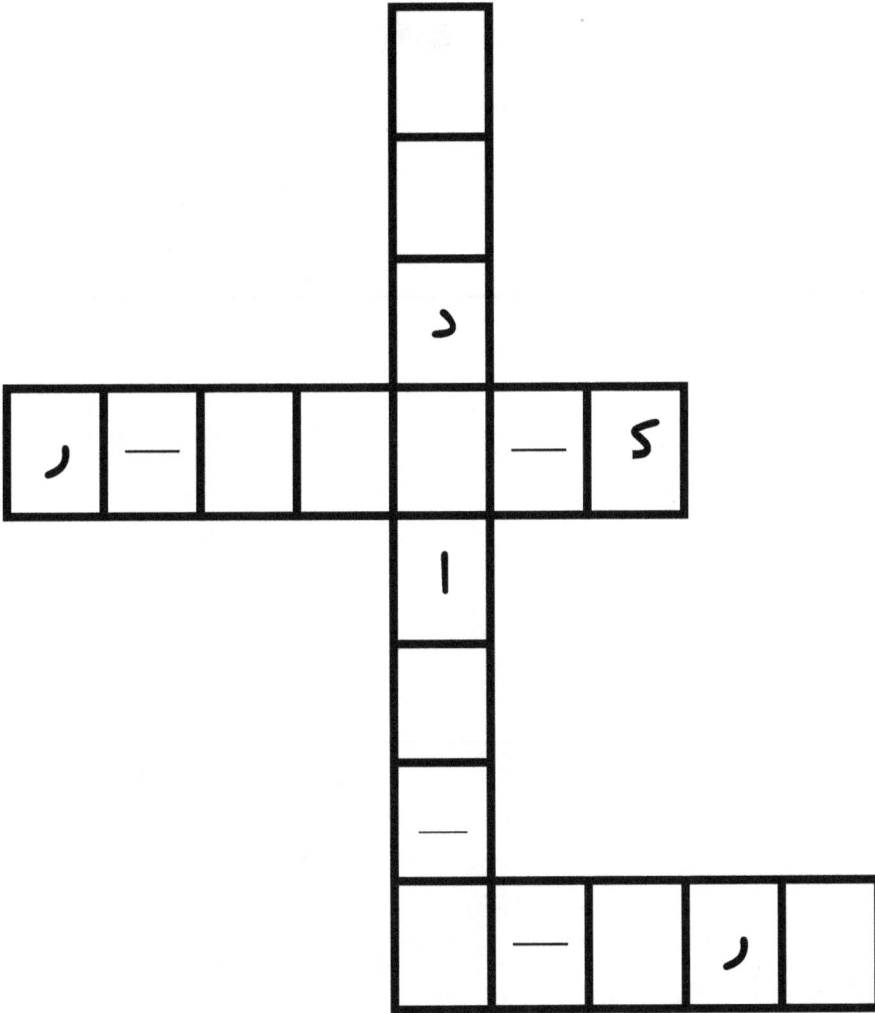

Find the word below in the puzzle.   کلمه زیر را در جدول پیدا کن.

کَبوتَر

ن	م	د	کَ	ز	و	ل
ش	ن	و	بِ	ل	ا	کِ
تَ	ز	ا	و	بِ	گِ	ا
بِ	ت	ر	تَ	و	ه	خ
ک	ا	ل	ر	د	ا	کُ

Look at this picture and write its name under it.   به این شکل نگاه کن و اسمش را زیر آن بنویس.

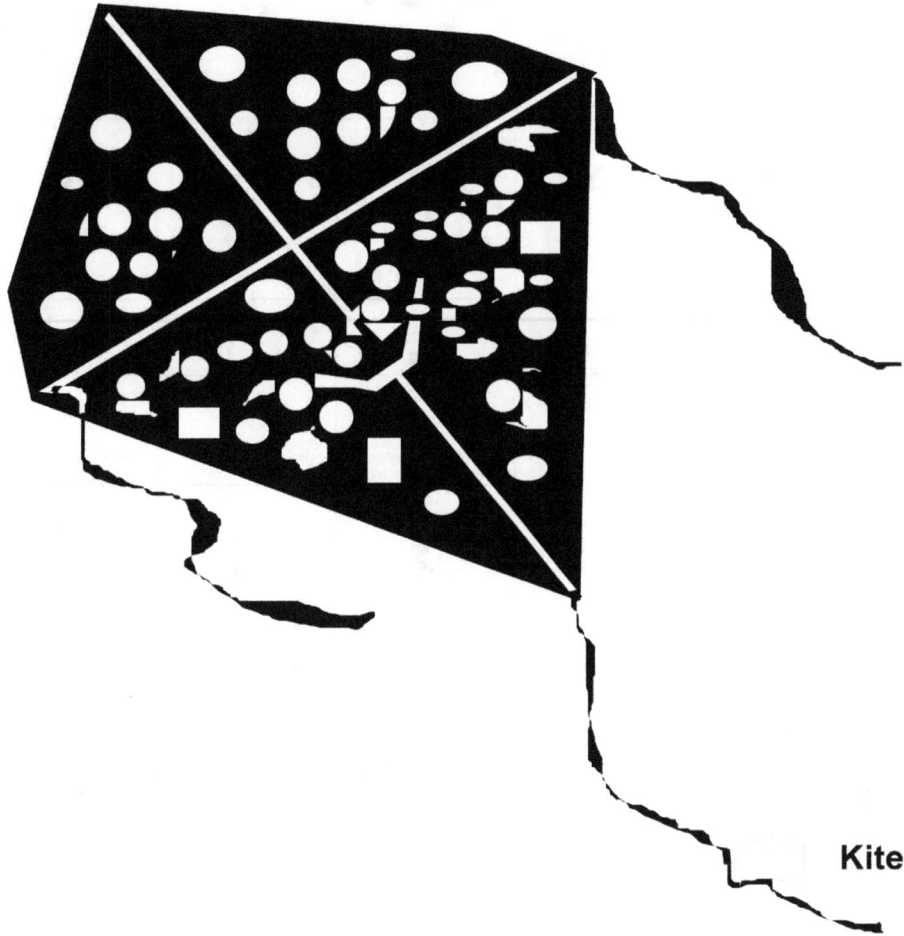

Kite

_____

اُردَک = __ + __ + __ + __ + __

کَبوتَر = __ + __ + __ + __ + __ + __ + __

بادبادَک = __ + __ + __ + __ + __ + __ + __ + __

Read the word below and draw a picture of it.   کلمه زیر را بخوان و شکلش را بکش.

اُردَک

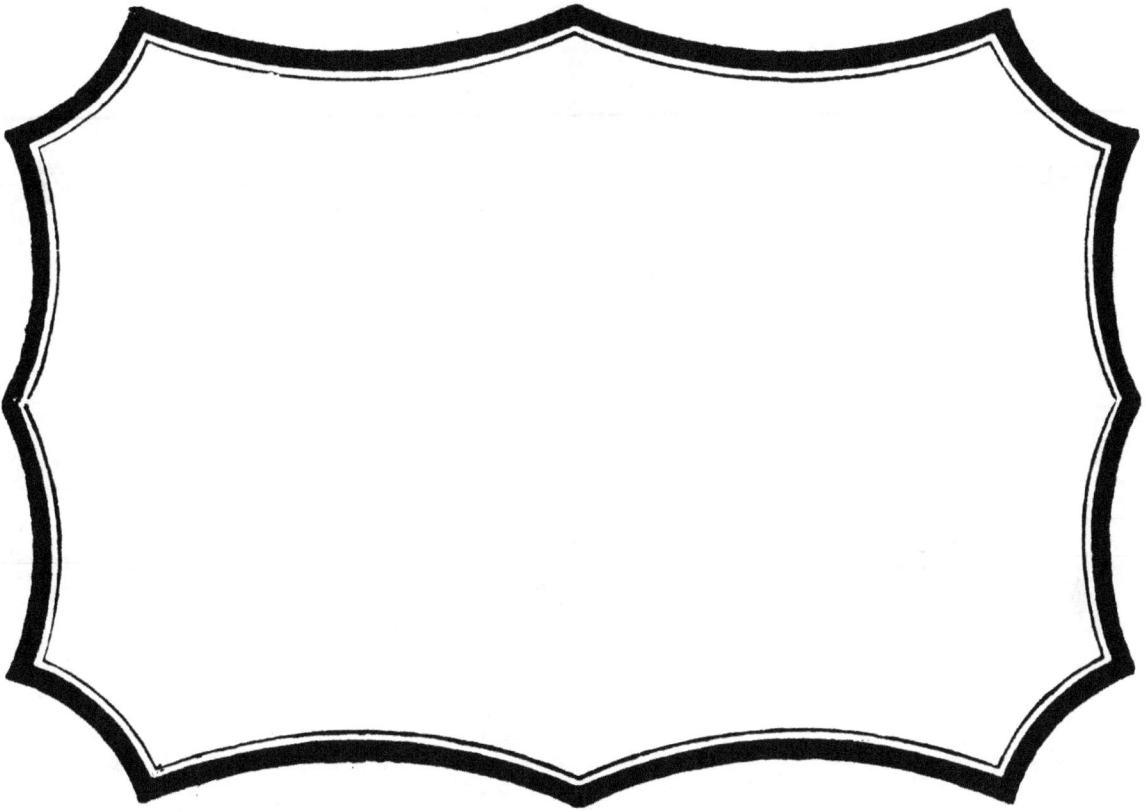

Exercise 7

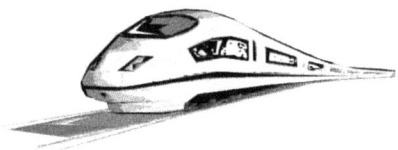

Train

تِرَن

(te. ran)

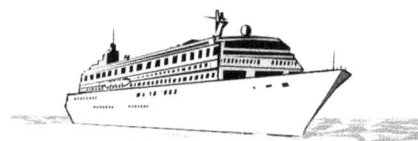

Ship

کَشتی

(kash. tee)

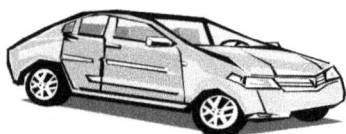

Car

ماشین

(maa. sheen)

Read the word for each picture and
write the letters in their places.

با کمک شکل ها، هر کلمه را بخوان و
صداهایش را در جدولِ روبرویش بنویس.

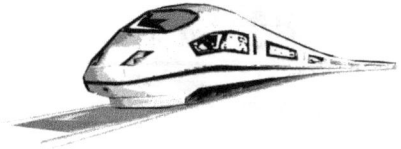

Train

تِرَن

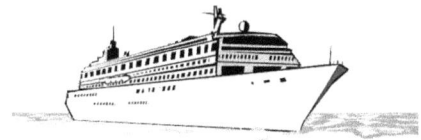

Ship

گَشتی

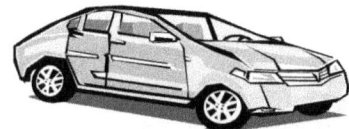

Car

ماشین

Connect each word to its picture.

هر کلمه را به شکلش وصل کن.

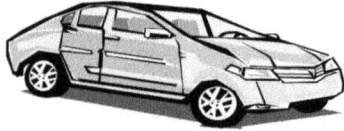

Car

کَشتی

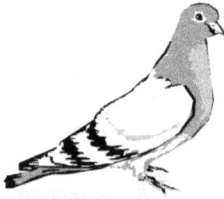

Pigeon

بادبادَک

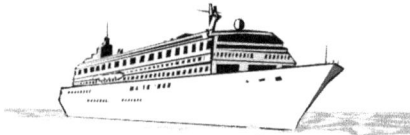

Ship

تِرَن

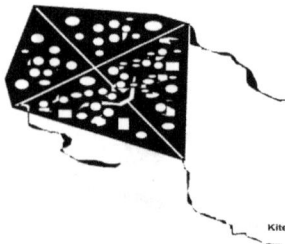

Kite

کَبوتَر

ماشین

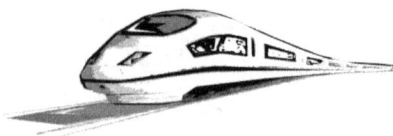

Train

Read the word for each picture and
write the letters in the puzzle.

با کمک شکل ها، هر کلمه را بخوان و
جایش را در جدول پیدا کن.

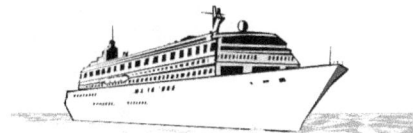

Ship

گَشتی

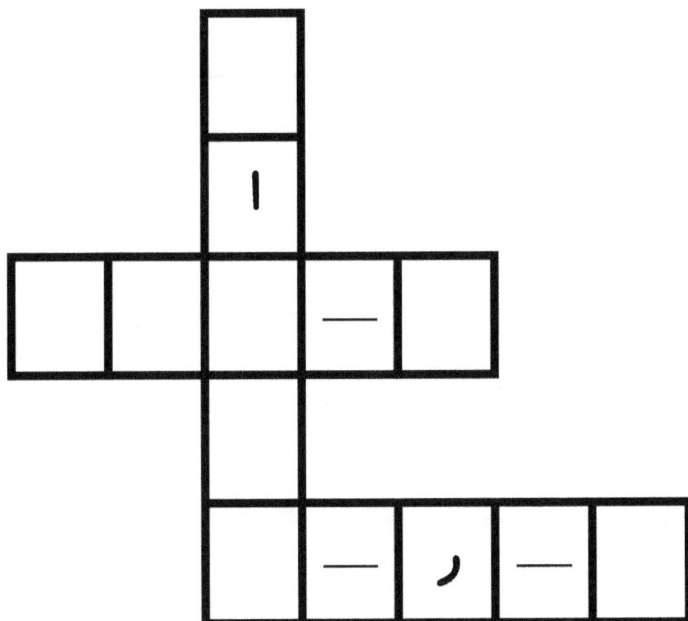

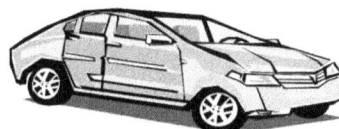

Car

ماشین

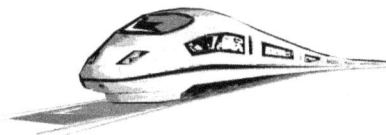

Train

تِرَن

Find the word below in the puzzle.

کلمه زیر را در جدول پیدا کن.

کَشتی

و	ا	ض	ب	ل	زِ	ج
د	ا	تِ	ل	ز	ا	ه
ش	ی	ت	ش	گَ	شا	ا
ت	ی	ی	ا	د	ا	تِ
ف	ط	دُ	ه	رَ	ش	گَ

۶۵

Look at this picture and write its name under it.   به این شکل نگاه کن و اسمش را زیر آن بنویس.

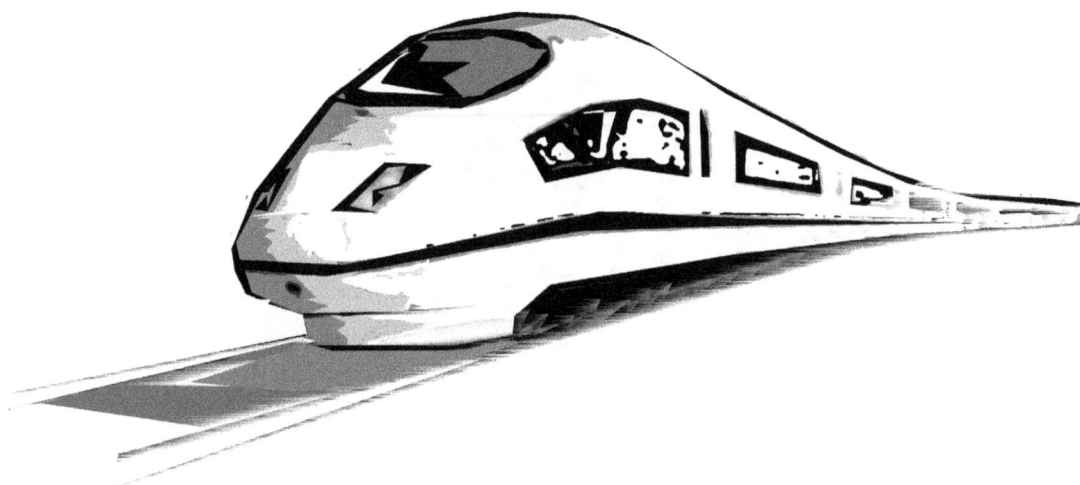

Train

_____

Write the letters for each word.   صداهای هر کلمه را بنویس.

___ + ___ + ___ + ___ + ___ = تِرَن

___ + ___ + ___ + ___ + ___ = کَشتی

___ + ___ + ___ + ___ + ___ = ماشین

Read the word below and draw a picture of it.   کلمه زیر را بخوان و شکلش را بکش.

ماشین

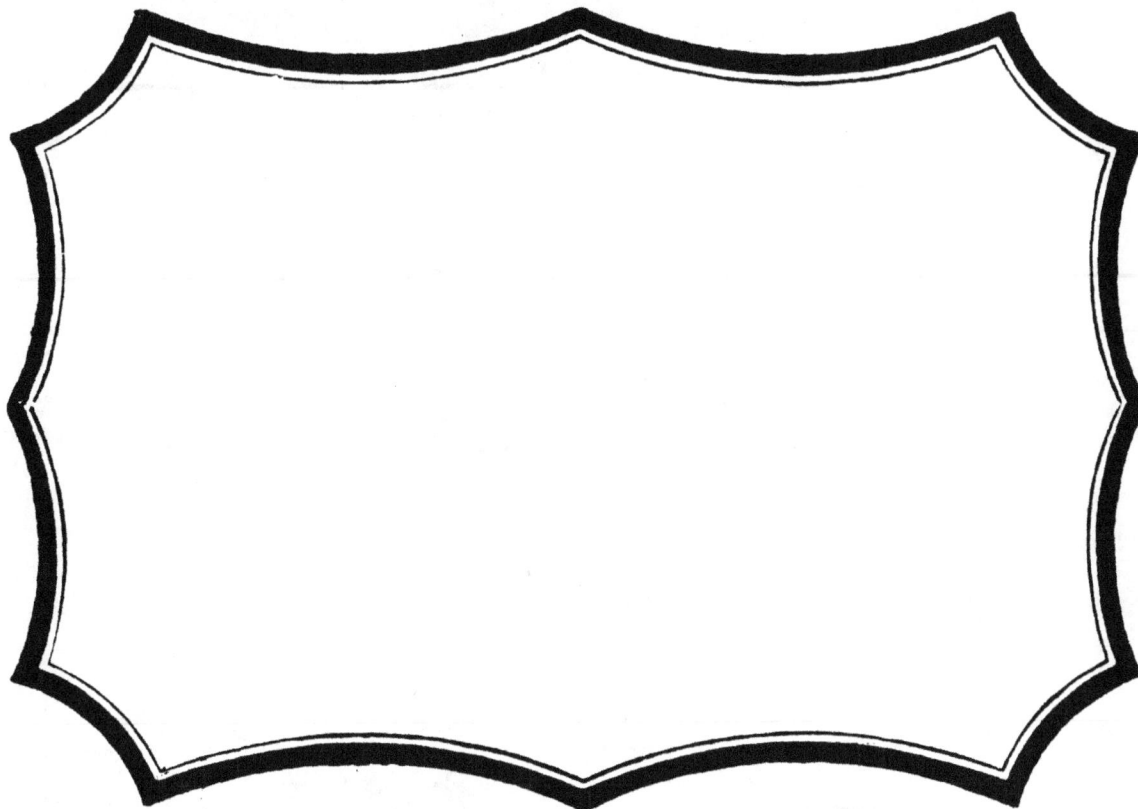

Exercise 8

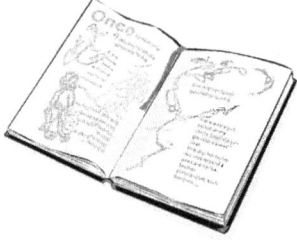

كِتاب

(ke. taab)

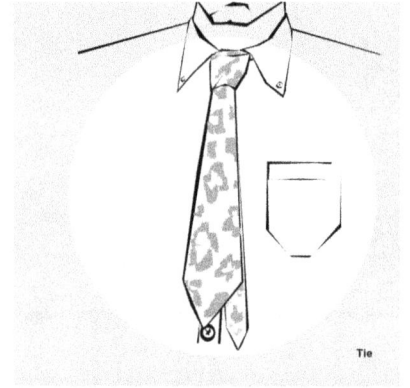

كِراوات

(ke. raa. vaat)

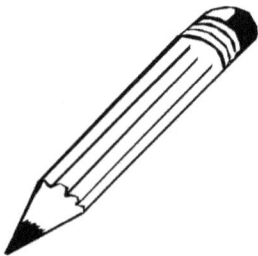

مِداد

(me. daad)

Read the word for each picture and
write the letters in their places.

با کمک شکل ها، هر کلمه را بخوان و
صداهایش را در جدولِ روبرویش بنویس.

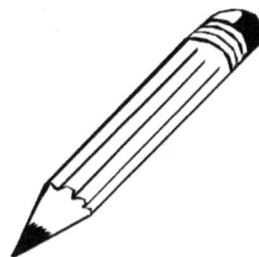

Pencil

مِداد

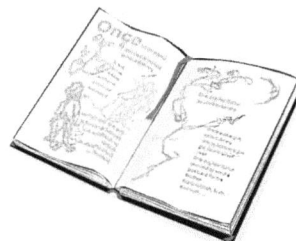

Book

کِتاب

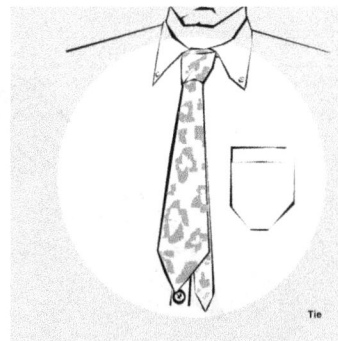

Tie

کِراوات

۷۰

Connect each word to its picture.

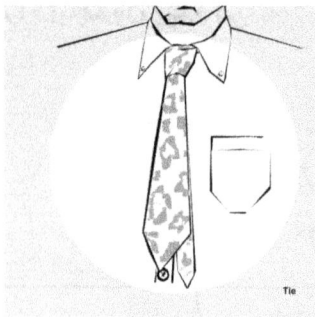

Tie

کِتاب

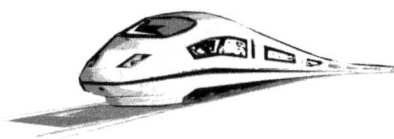

Train

کَشتی

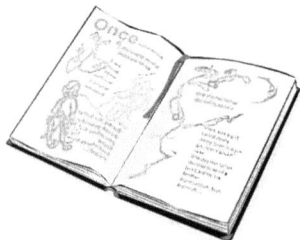

Book

مِداد

تِرَن

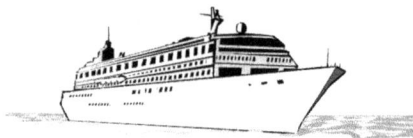

Ship

کِراوات

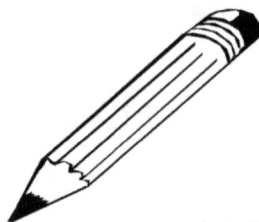

Pencil

Read the word for each picture and
write the letters in the puzzle.

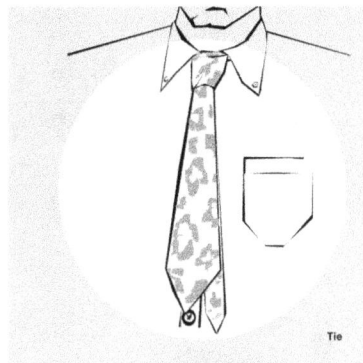

کِراوات

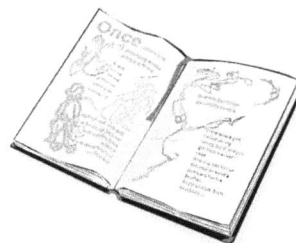

کِتاب

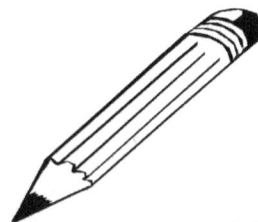

مِداد

با کمک شکل ها، هر کلمه را بخوان و جایش
را در جدول پیدا کن.

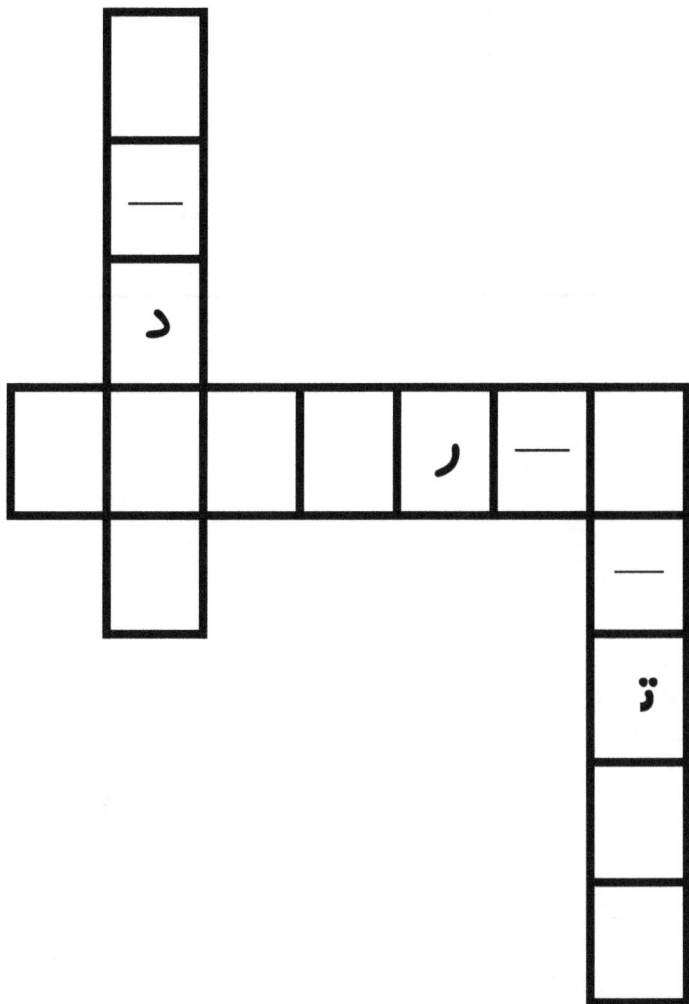

Find the word below in the puzzle.

کلمه زیر را در جدول پیدا کن.

کِتاب

م	کِ	و	ا	ه	ر
ش	تِ	گُ	ه	تَ	ن
ه	ا	ل	ر	گَ	ا
س	ب	یِ	گ	د	ز

Look at this picture and write its name under it.   به این شکل نگاه کن و اسمش را زیر آن بنویس.

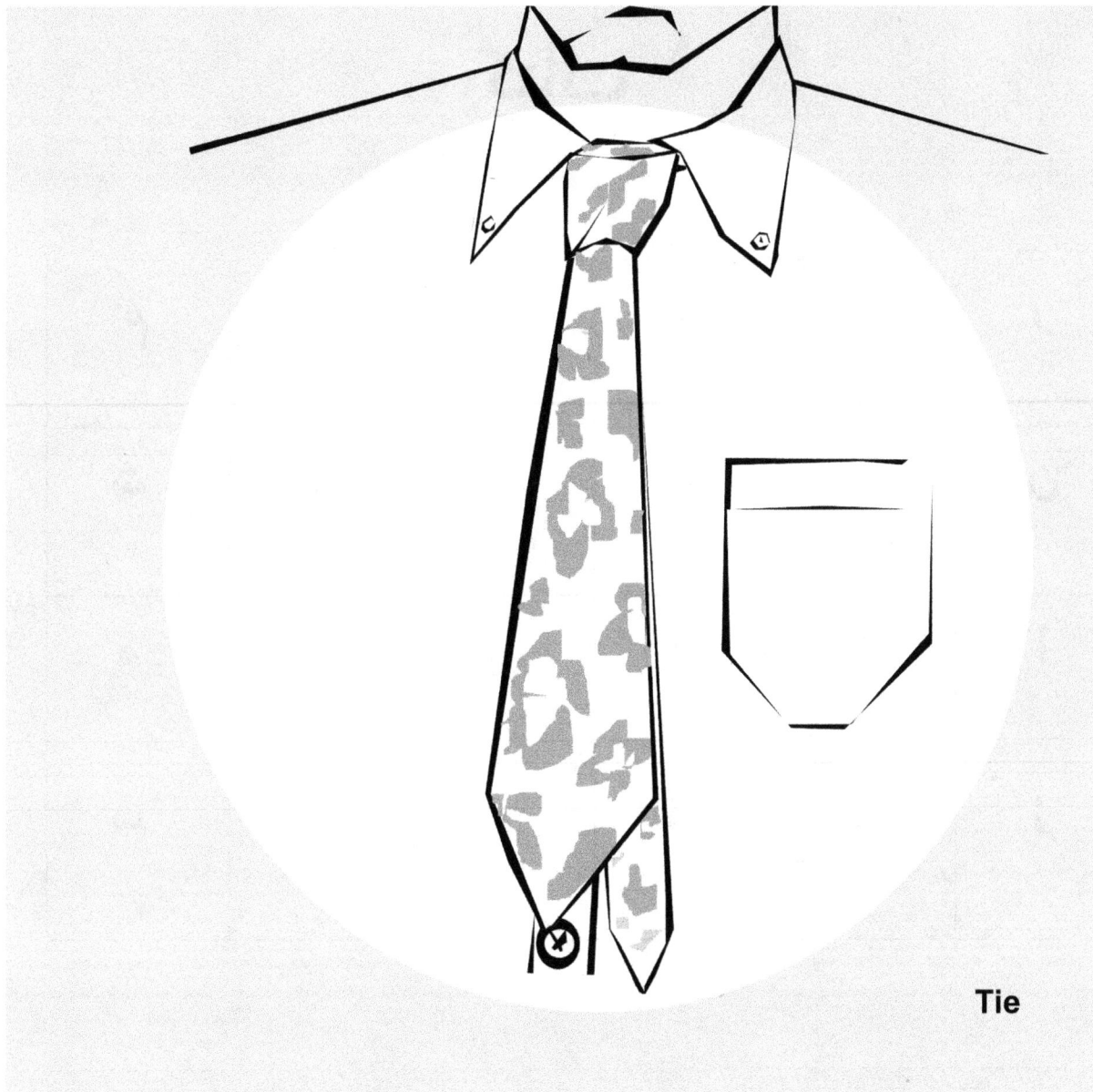

Tie

_____

Write the letters for each word. صداهای هر کلمه را بنویس.

کِتاب= ___ + ___ + ___ + ___ + ___ + ___

مِداد= ___ + ___ + ___ + ___ + ___ + ___

کِراوات= ___ + ___ + ___ + ___ + ___ + ___ + ___ + ___

Read the word below and draw a picture of it.   کلمه زیر را بخوان و شکلش را بکش.

مِداد

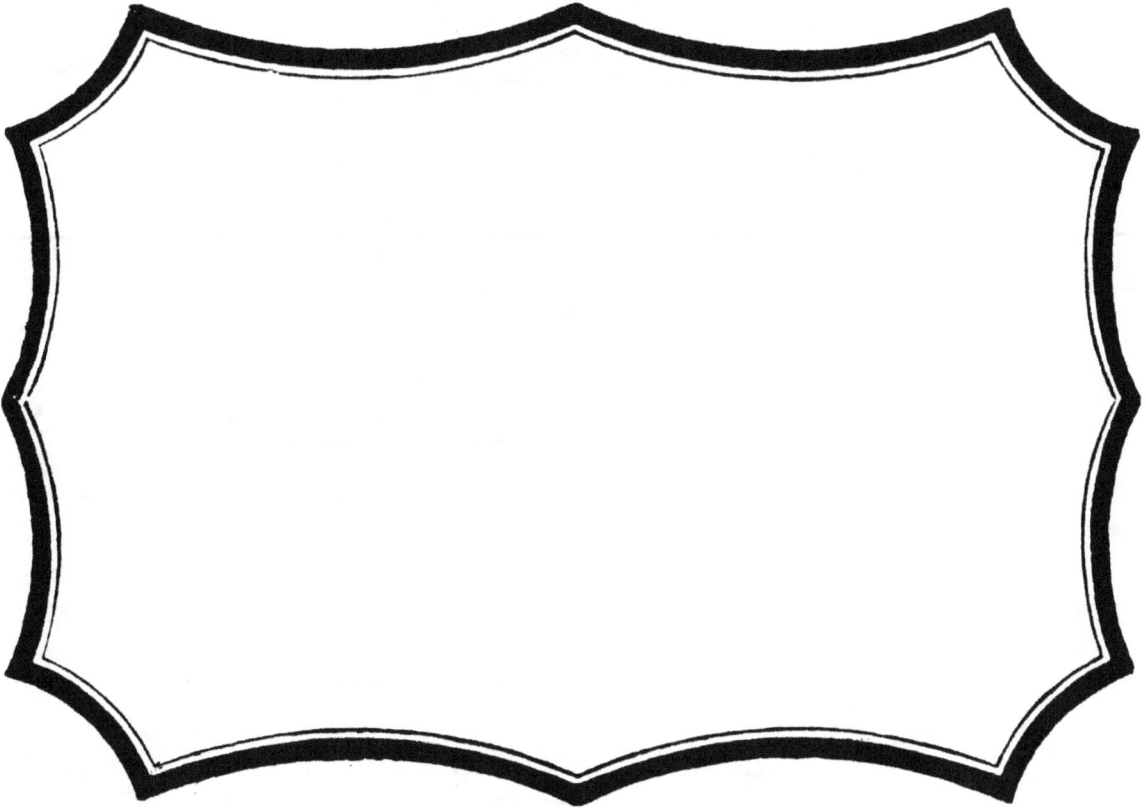

Exercise 9

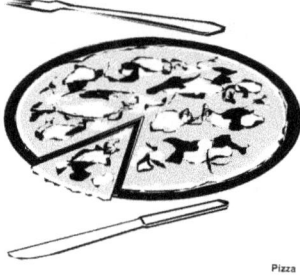

Pizza

پیتزا

(peet. zaa)

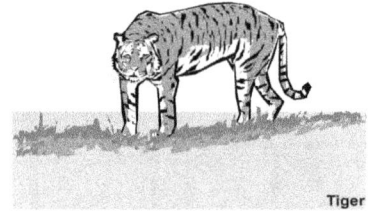

Tiger

بَبر

(babr)

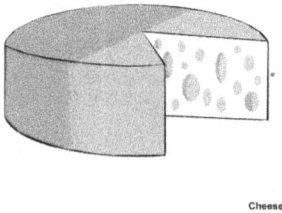

Cheese

پَنیر

(pa .neer)

۷۷

Read the word for each picture and
write the letters in their places.

با کمک شکل ها، هر کلمه را بخوان و

صداهایش را در جدولِ روبرویش بنویس.

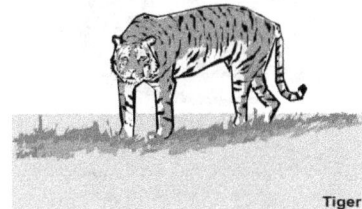
Tiger

بَبر

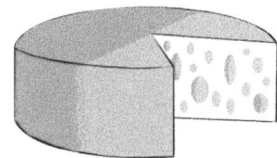
Cheese

پَنیر

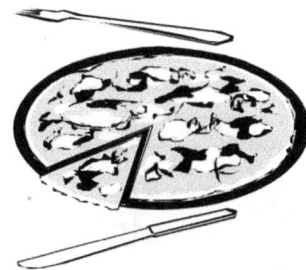
Pizza

پیتزا

۷۸

Connect each word to its picture.

هر کلمه را به شکلش وصل کن.

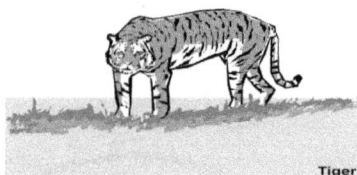

Tiger

پیتزا

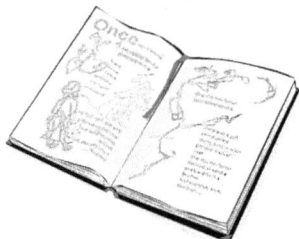

Book

مِداد

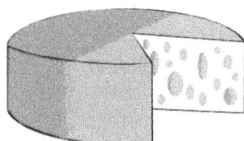

Cheese

پَنیر

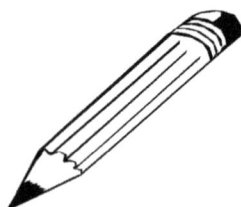

Pencil

کِتاب

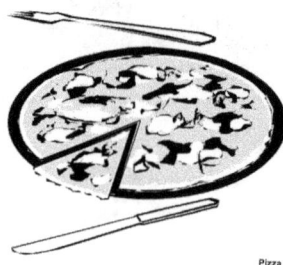

Pizza

بَبر

Read the word for each picture and
write the letters in the puzzle.

با کمک شکل ها، هر کلمه را بخوان و
جایش را در جدول پیدا کن.

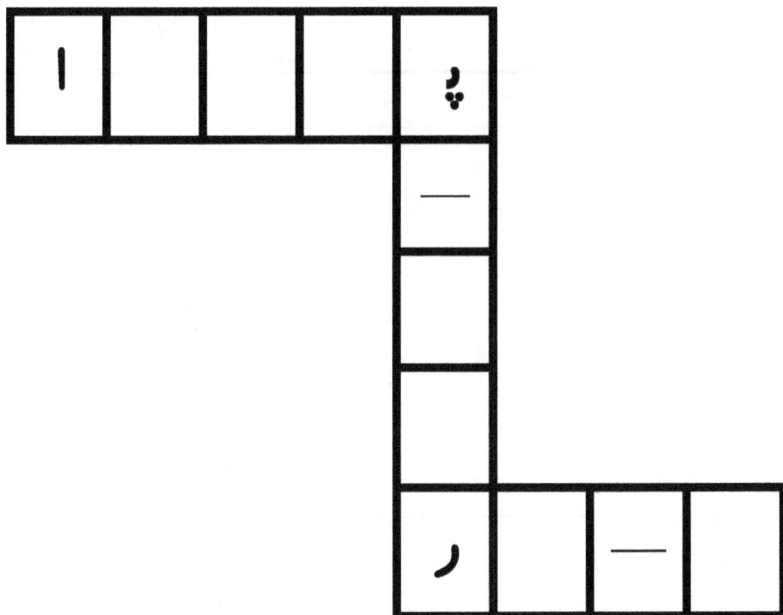

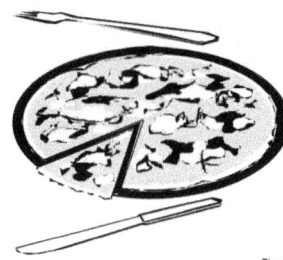

پیتزا

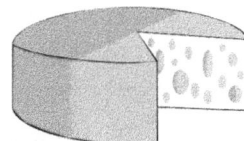

پَنیر

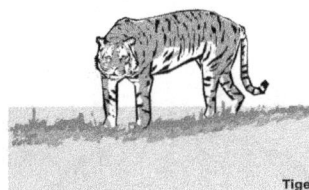

بَبر

Find the word below in the puzzle.

كلمه زير را در جدول پيدا كن.

بَبر

ب	ه	و	ر	ه	ا	تُ
ا	ر	ت	م	ا	ت	بِ
ک	س	بَ	ا	ذ	و	م
و	ه	ر	بِ	بَ	ر	ک
ن	م	ز	تِ	گ	ت	ا

Look at this picture and write its name under it.   به این شکل نگاه کن و اسمش را زیر آن بنویس.

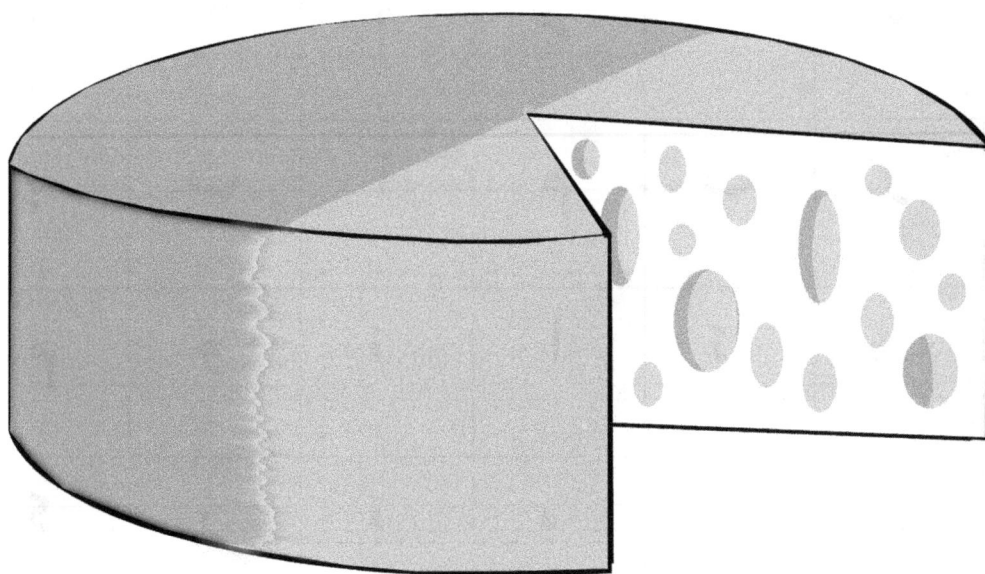

Cheese

_____

صداهای هر کلمه را بنویس.

Write the letters for each word.

بَبر= __ + __ + __ + __

پَنیر= __ + __ + __ + __ + __

پیتزا= __ + __ + __ + __ + __

Read the word below and draw a picture of it. کلمه زیر را بخوان و شکلش را بکش.

پیتزا

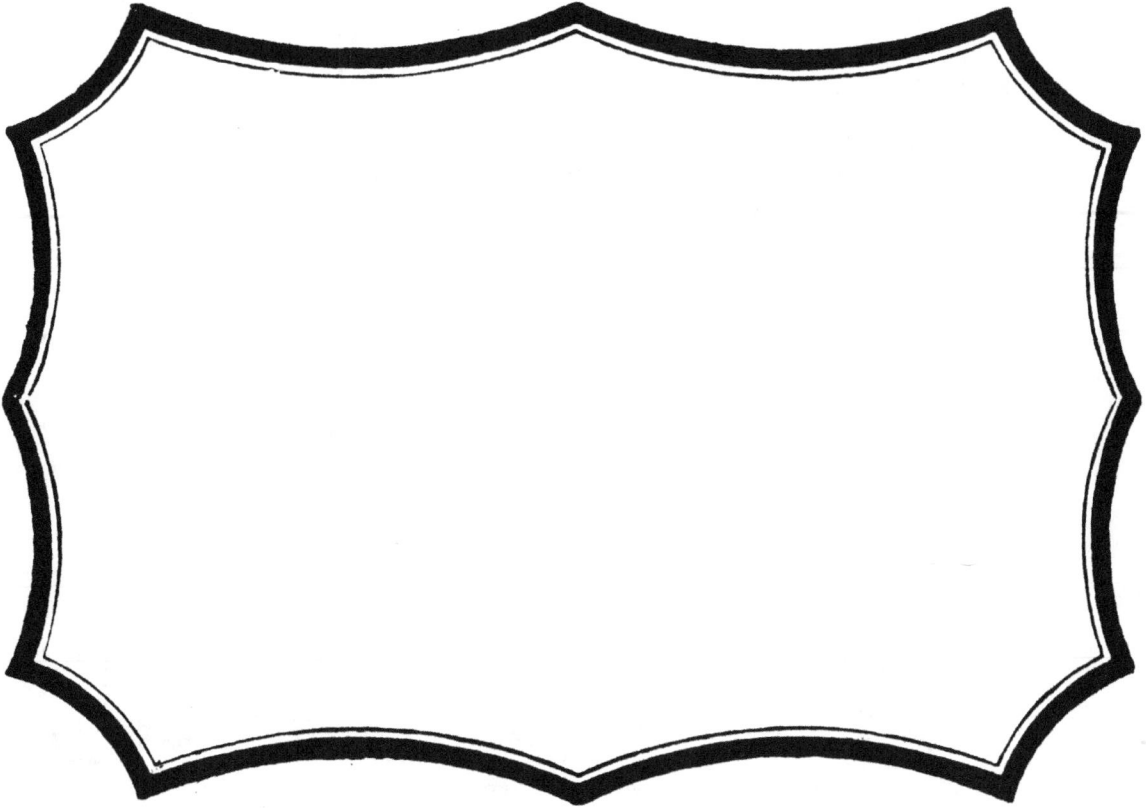

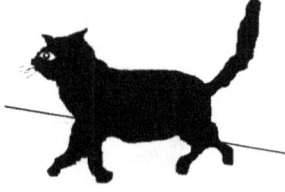

Cat

گُربه

(gor. be)

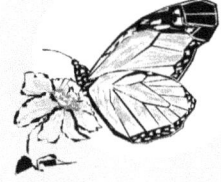

Butterfly

پَروانه

(par. vaa. ne)

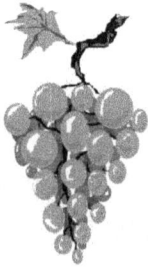

Grapes

اَنگور

(an. goor)

Read the word for each picture and
write the letters in their places.

با کمک شکل ها، هر کلمه را بخوان و
صداهایش را در جدولِ روبرویش بنویس.

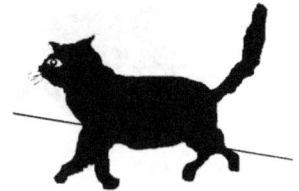

Cat

گُربه

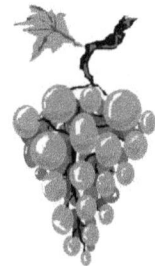

Grapes

آنگور

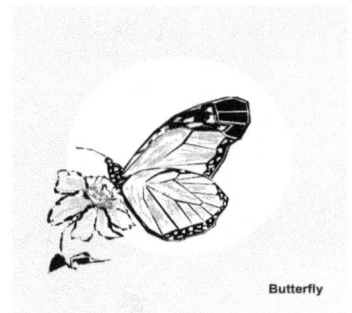

Butterfly

پَروانه

Connect each word to its picture.

هر کلمه را به شکلش وصل کن.

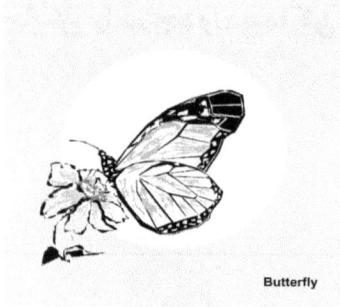
Butterfly

آنگور

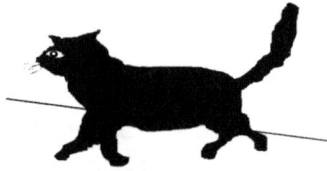
Cat

پَروانه

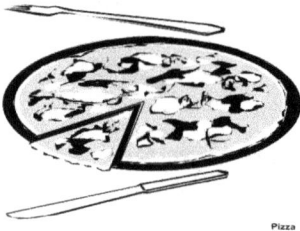
Pizza

بَبر

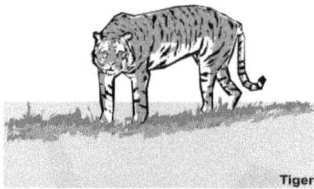
Tiger

گُربه

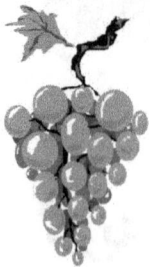
Grapes

پیتزا

Read the word for each picture and
write the letters in the puzzle.

با کمک شکل ها، هر کلمه را بخوان و
جایش را در جدول پیدا کن.

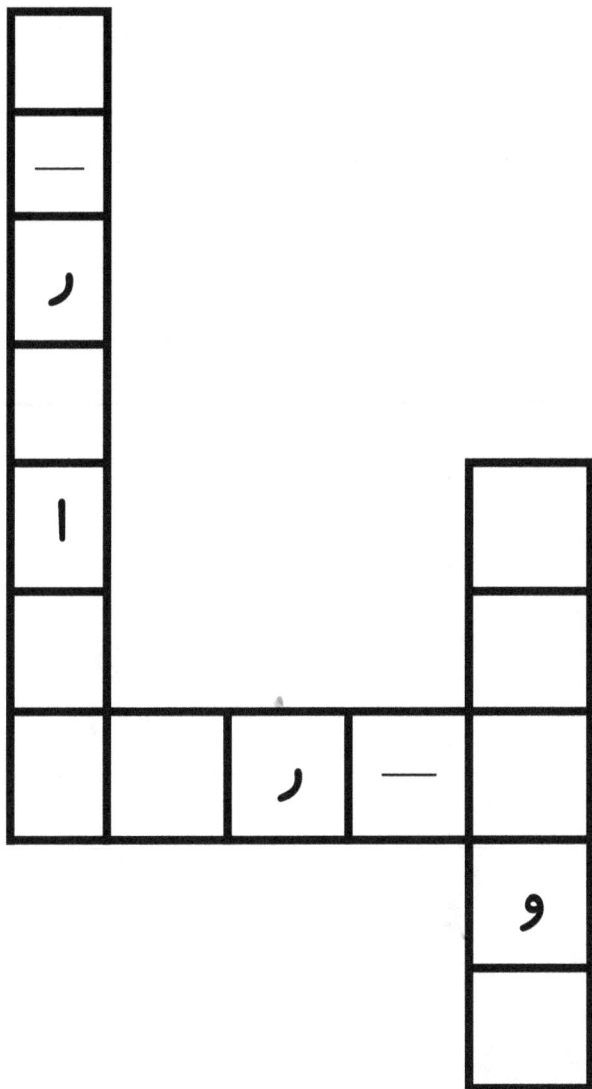

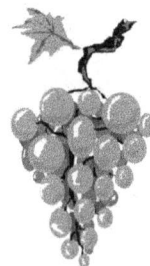

Grapes

آنگور

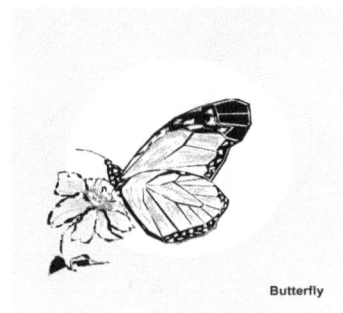

Butterfly

پَروانه

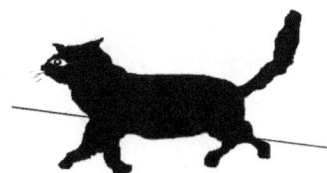

Cat

گُربه

Find the word below in the puzzle.

کلمه زیر را در جدول پیدا کن.

پَروانه

پَ	ر	و	ا	ز	ه
ا	س	یـ	ن	د	پ
پَ	ا	ک	م	ز	و
و	م	یـ	ی	ن	ه

Look at this picture and write its name under it.   به این شکل نگاه کن و اسمش را زیر آن بنویس.

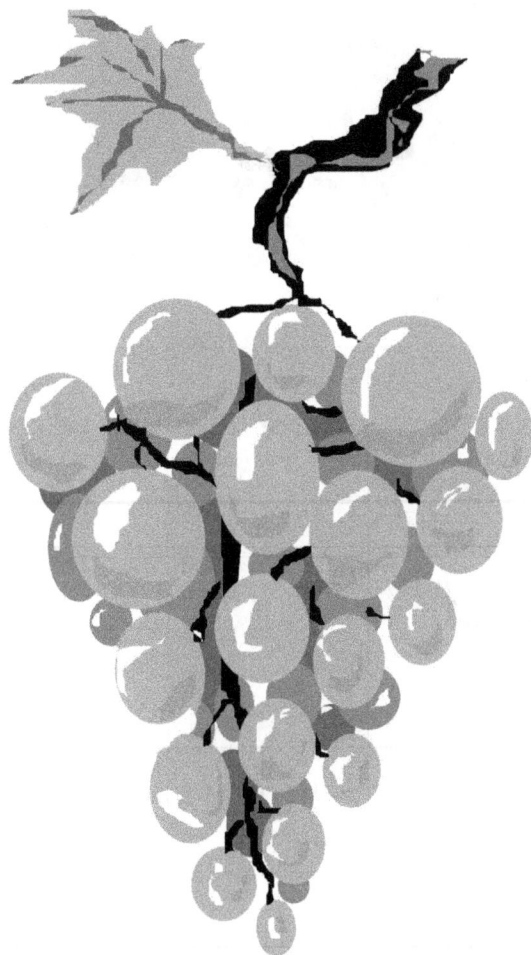

Grapes

_____

Write the letters for each word.   صداهای هر کلمه را بنویس.

__ + __ + __ + __ + __ = گُربه

__ + __ + __ + __ + __ = آنگور

__ + __ + __ + __ + __ + __ + __ = پَروانه

Read the word below and draw a picture of it.   کلمه زیر را بخوان و شکلش را بکش.

گُربه

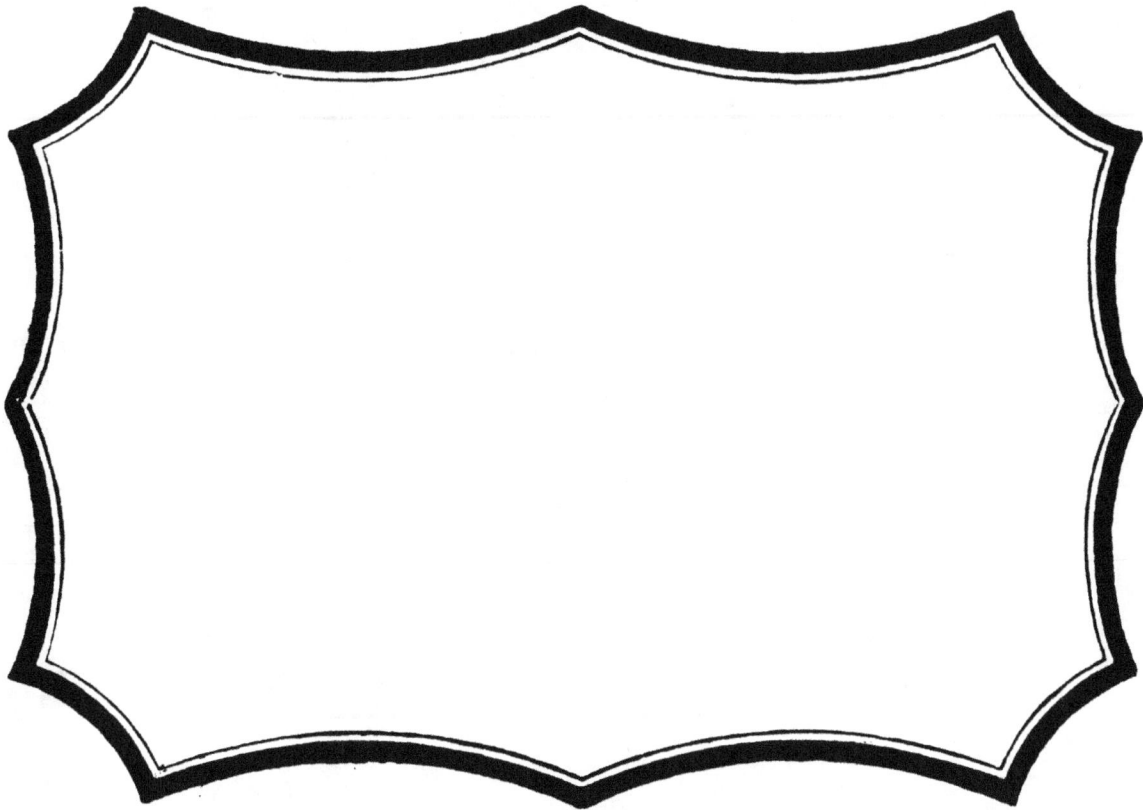

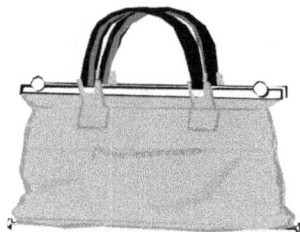

Bag

کیف

(keef)

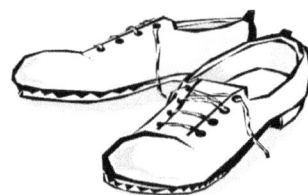

Shoes

کَفش

(kafsh)

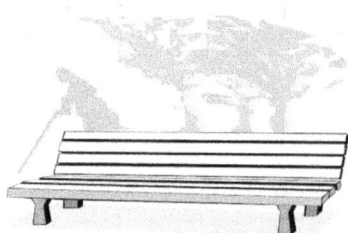

Bench

نیمکَت

(neem. kat)

Read the word for each picture and write the letters in their places.

با کمک شکل ها، هر کلمه را بخوان و
صداهایش را در جدولِ روبرویش بنویس.

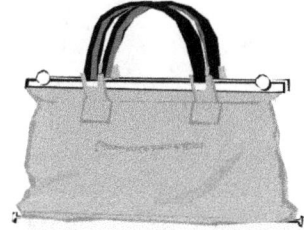

Bag

کیف

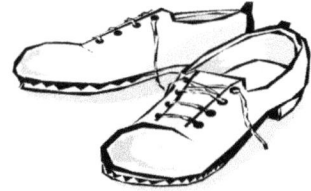

Shoes

کَفش

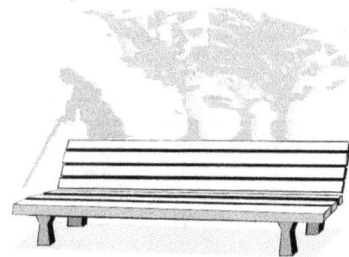

Bench

نیمکَت

Connect each word to its picture.

هر کلمه را به شکلش وصل کن.

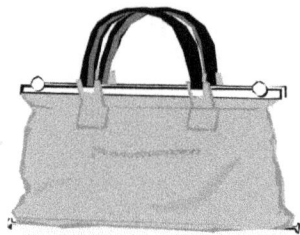

Bag

كيف

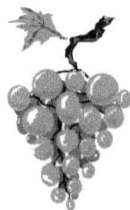

Grapes

گُربه

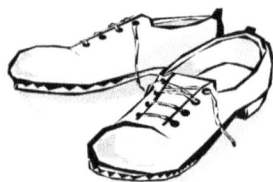

Shoes

نیمکَت

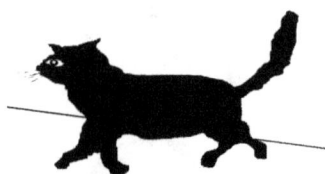

Cat

آنگور

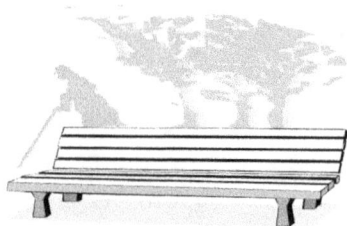

Bench

كَفش

Read the word for each picture and
write the letters in the puzzle.

با کمک شکل ها، هر کلمه را بخوان و
جایش را در جدول پیدا کن.

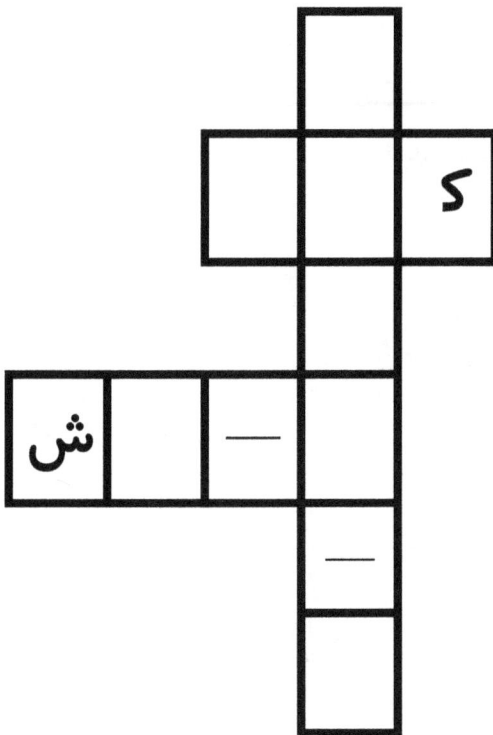

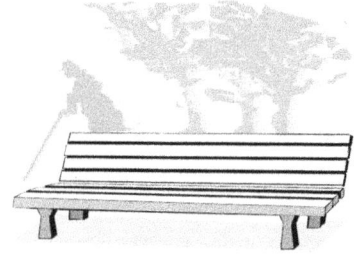

Bench

نیمکَت

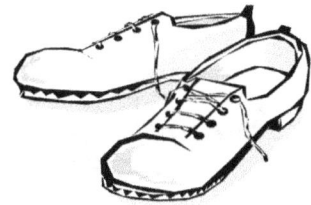

Shoes

کَفش

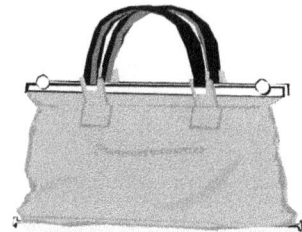

Bag

کیف

Find the word below in the puzzle.

کلمه زیر را در جدول پیدا کن.

نیمکَت

ن	ب	د	ذ	ز	و	ل
ش	ا	و	يِ	ل	ا	گَ
تَ	ذ	ا	م	بِ	گِ	ا
بِ	م	ر	گَ	و	ه	خ
ک	ا	ل	ت	کِ	ا	گُ

Look at this picture and write its name under it.   به این شکل نگاه کن و اسمش را زیر آن بنویس.

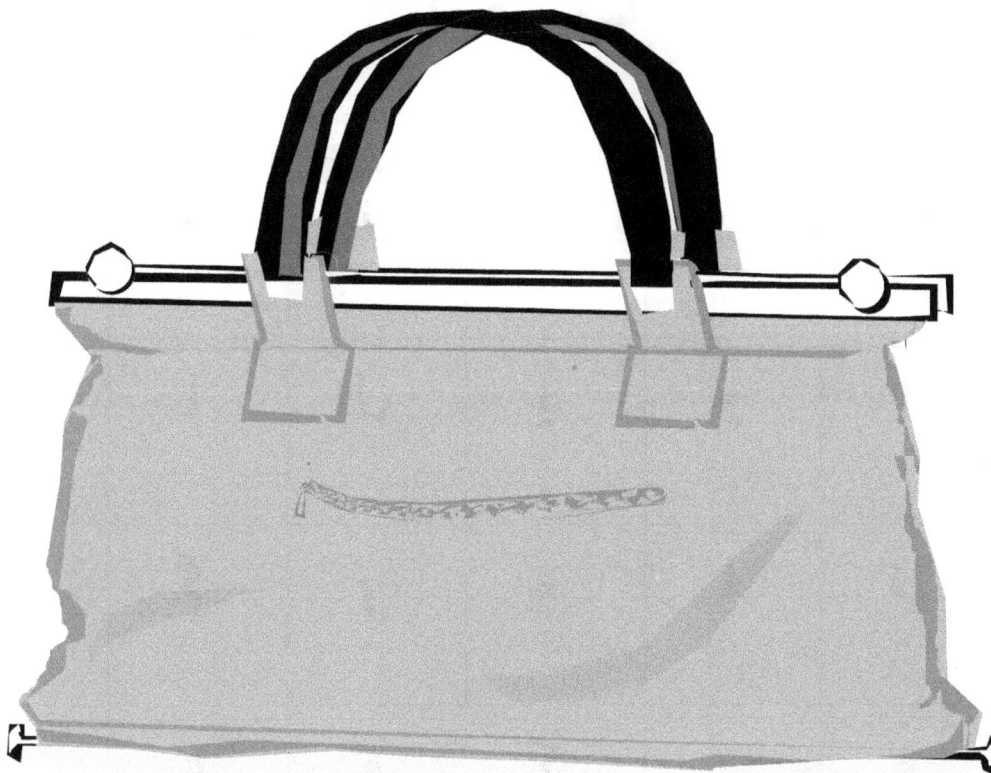

Bag

_____

Write the letters for each word.

صداهای هر کلمه را بنویس.

کیف = __ + __ + __

کَفش = __ + __ + __ + __

نیمکَت = __ + __ + __ + __ + __ + __

۹۹

Read the word below and draw a picture of it.   کلمه زیر را بخوان و شکلش را بکش.

کَفش

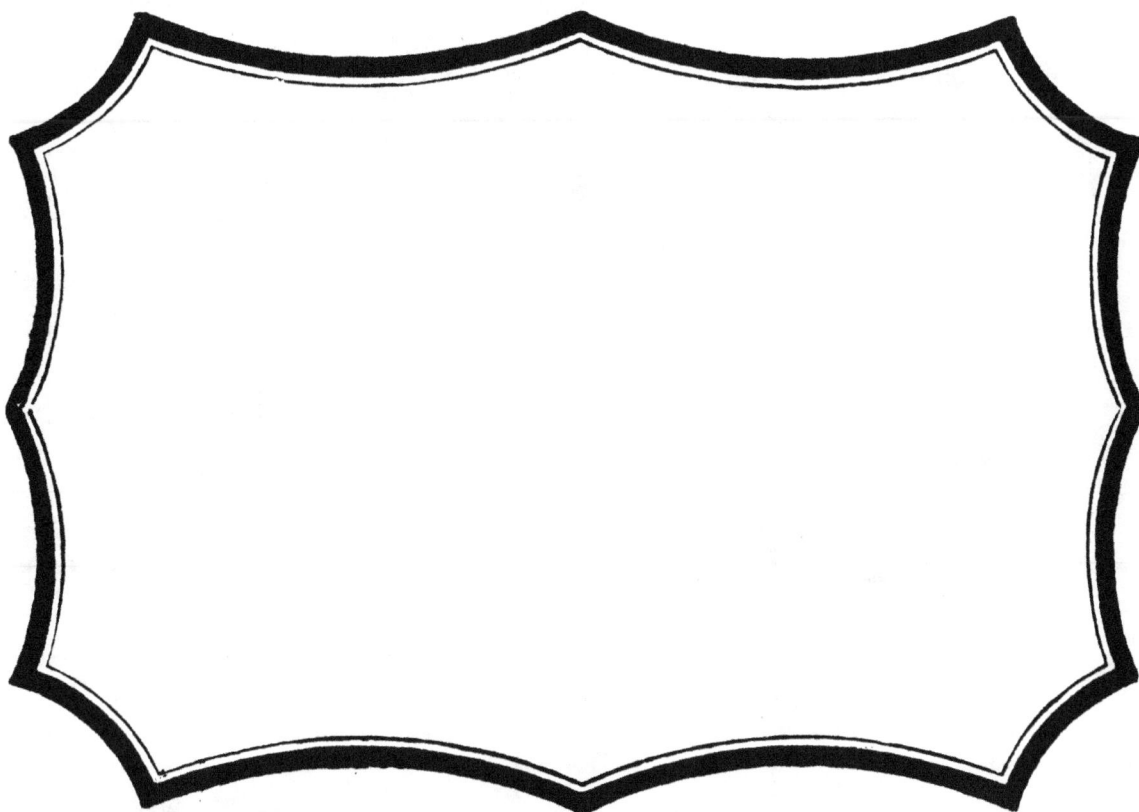

Exercise 12

تمرین ۱۲

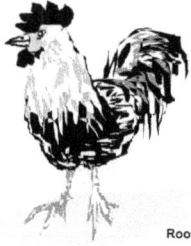

Rooster

خُروس

(ǩo. roos)

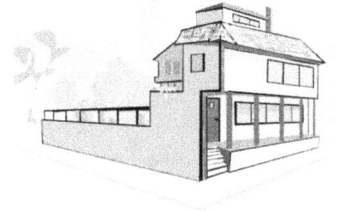

House

ساختِمان

(saak̆. te. maan)

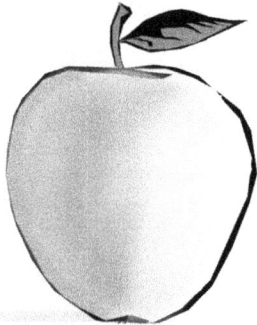

Apple

سیب

(seeb)

Read the word for each picture and
write the letters in their places.

با کمک شکل ها، هر کلمه را بخوان و
صداهایش را در جدولِ روبرویش بنویس.

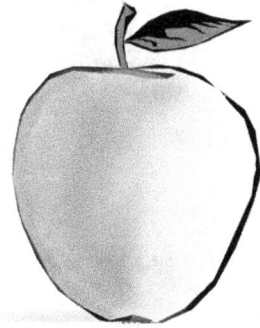

Apple

سیب

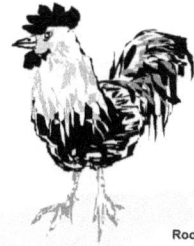

Rooster

خُروس

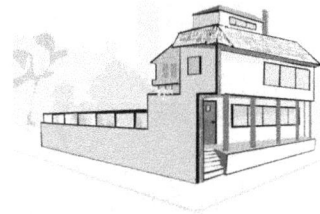

House

ساختِمان

Connect each word to its picture.

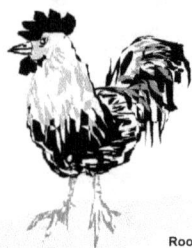

Rooster

ساختِمان

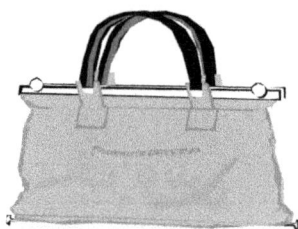

Bag

کَفش

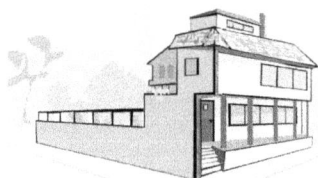

House

سیب

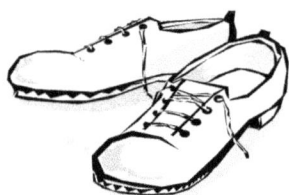

Shoes

کیف

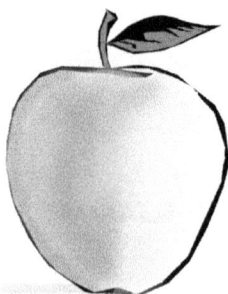

Apple

خُروس

Read the word for each picture and
write the letters in the puzzle.

با کمک شکل ها، هر کلمه را بخوان و
جایش را در جدول پیدا کن.

Rooster

خُروس

House

ساختِمان

Apple

سیب

ا

ر ــ

ــ

ن

Find the word below in the puzzle.

کلمه زیر را در جدول پیدا کن.

خُروس

س	خُ	ن	و	ل	ه	ف
م	ر	ل	ذ	اُ	ﺯ	و
ا	و	س	ن	خُ	ل	ه
ر	س	ن	گ	ی	اِ	ل
اَ	ر	ذ	ب	ص	و	پ

Look at this picture and write its name under it.   به این شکل نگاه کن و اسمش را زیر آن بنویس.

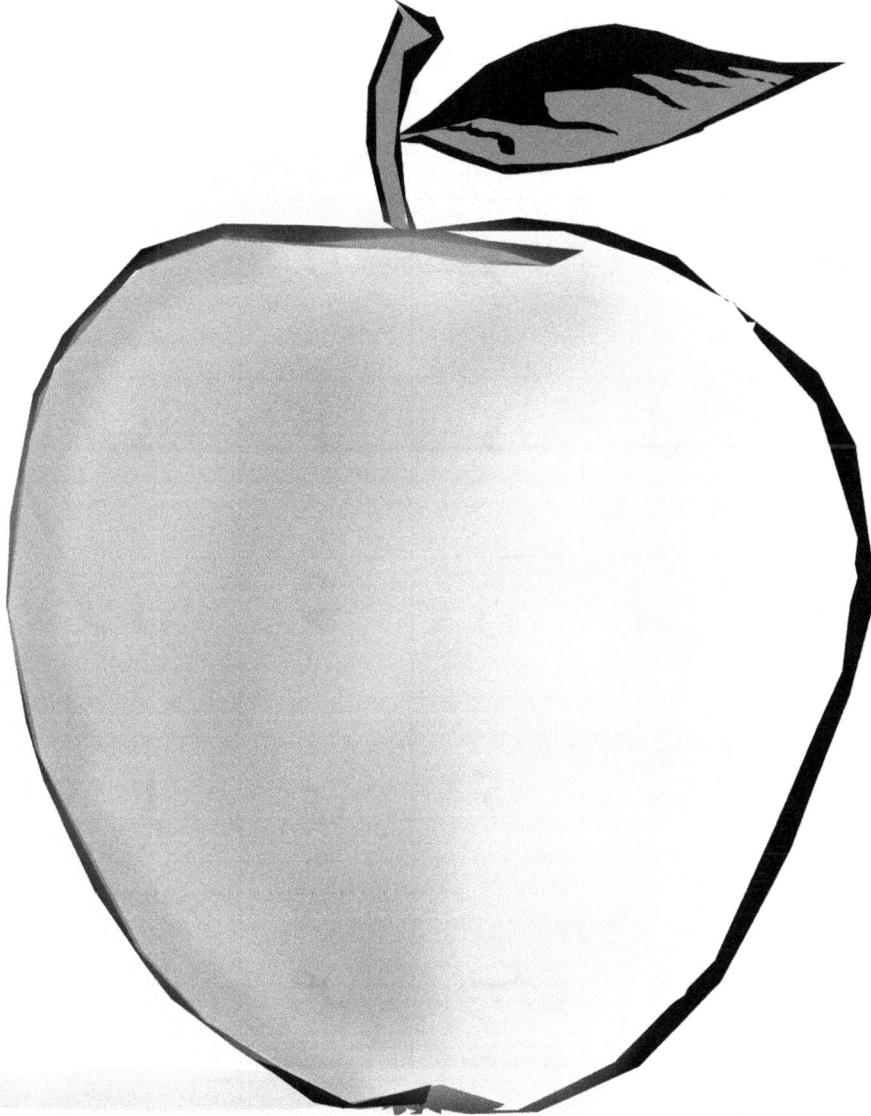

Apple

———————————————

Write the letters for each word. صداهای هر کلمه را بنویس.

سیب = __ + __ + __

خُروس = __ + __ + __ + __ + __

ساختِمان = __ + __ + __ + __ + __ + __ + __ + __

Read the word below and draw a picture of it. کلمه زیر را بخوان و شکلش را بکش.

ساختِمان

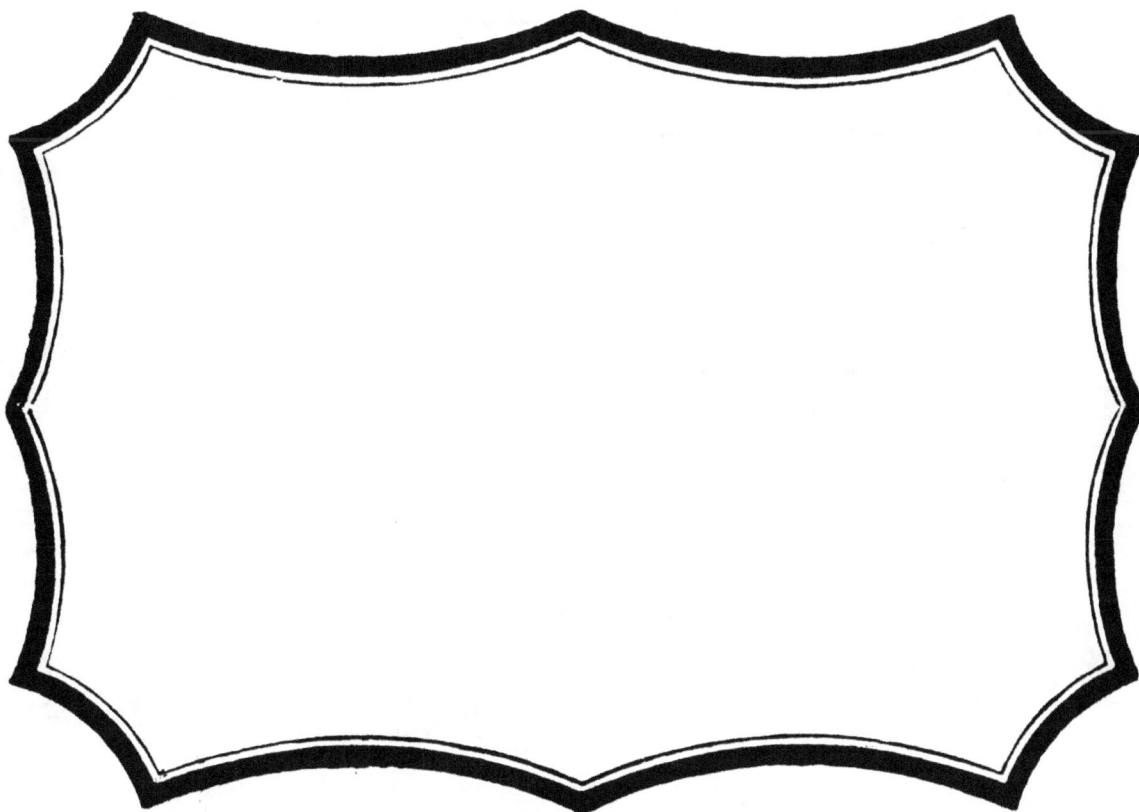

برای آشنایی با سایر کتاب های " نشر بهار " از وب سایت این انتشارات

دیدن فرمائید.

**To learn more about the other publications of Bahar Books
please visit the website.**

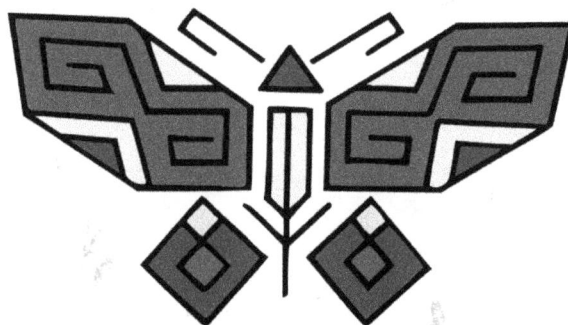

Bahar Books

www.baharbooks.com